Rocky Mountain Cuisine Cookbook

ROCKY

Fresh foods

MOUNTAIN

from the kitchens

CUISINE

of Canadian

COOKBOOK

Rocky Mountain Resorts

HUBERT AUMEIER

Random House of Canada

Random House of Canada, Ltd.
33 Yonge Street, Suite 210
Toronto, Ontario
M5E 1G4

Canadian Cataloguing in Publication Data

Aumeier, Hubert
   The Rocky Mountain cuisine cookbook

Includes index.
ISBN 0–679–30836–9

1. Cookery, Canadian – British Columbia style. 2. Cookery, Canadian – Alberta style.
3. Cookery – Rocky Mountains, Canadian (B.C. and Alta.). 4. Cookery (Natural foods).
5. Cookery (Wild foods). I. Title

TX715.6.A95 1997   641.59711   C96–931600–3

Packager: Susan Yates & Victor Levin/INFACT Publishing Ltd.

Design: Andrew Smith

Page layout and composition: Joseph Gisini/Andrew Smith Graphics Inc.

Front cover illustration: Bill Russell

Interior illustrations: Valerie St. Denis

Editor: Mary Adachi

Recipe Testing: Maureen Lollar

Printed and bound in Canada by Friesens

CONTENTS

Soups

Starters

Salads

Fish and Seafood

Meat and Game

Poultry

Side Dishes

Stocks, Condiments and Jams

Cookies and Bars

Desserts

ACKNOWLEDGEMENTS

I want to thank, in particular, Pat and Connie O'Connor, owners of Canadian Rocky Mountain Resorts for their passion and support of the culinary arts. It is wonderful working with both of them. I am indebted to my friend Bonnie Stern and her team for their encouragement and support in preparing this book; Carole Martin, who introduced me to cooking classes and always has good ideas; Shelly Gordash, the wonderful spirited host at Deer Lodge who was instrumental in giving Rocky Mountain Cuisine its name; David Forestell, former chef of Buffalo Mountain Lodge for his high standards, discipline, tremendous creativity and help in achieving the goals of Rocky Mountain Cuisine; Ken Canavan, chef at Cilantro for his never-ending ideas, dedication and love for unusual flavours; Walter von Rotz for his frankness, friendship and generously shared experience — not to forget all those delicious smoked and cured game products he created; Maureen Lollar for cheerfully testing all the recipes; all the chefs from our lodges and restaurants who shared their recipes and contributed ideas; Mary Adachi, for her careful editing and good humour; Susan Yates for making all this possible; Evelyn Zablosky for her appreciation of fine food, good coffee and everlasting smile; Rosemarie Enslin for her brilliant marketing; all the staff of Canadian Rocky Mountain Resorts who supported me on this project; Marlis, my lifetime companion, who ate successful and not-so-successful culinary experiments, for her honesty and moral support; and last, but not least, Resi, my mother, who was always in good spirits and who imparted to me, from early childhood, her knowledge of "wild" and simple foods.

INTRODUCTION

Cooking is such a rewarding and interesting profession. A good chef must be very dedicated, must love cooking and always be willing to learn, appreciate, discover, experiment and adapt while constantly seeking the fresh experience of preparing good and healthy food. But cooking good food can also be fascinating for the non-professional and for all who simply enjoy good food and read a cookbook like a novel.

A desire for perfection should be a quality every chef or home cook possesses. I believe that it is essential to pick the best possible ingredients, buy food in season and spend adequate time preparing, in a proper and respectful manner, these foods which nourish our body and soul. One should spend time examining food, smelling it, touching it, thinking about it, learning about it and being creative with it. Many of the recipes in the *Rocky Mountain Cuisine Cookbook* have been developed with a special regard for seasonal ingredients, healthy eating and preserving tradition. I do not recommend that chefs set out with a fixed recipe in mind that necessitates shopping for this or that special, hard-to-find ingredient. Instead, I encourage common sense.

The common-sense approach should also be used with the recipes in the *Rocky Mountain Cuisine Cookbook.* They don't have to be followed faithfully; you can be inspired by them and personalize them to your own taste. Feel free to make substitutions. There are some ingredients you may not find in your local stores and I have tried to offer alternatives for the unusual ones.

I grew up on a small farm in Bavaria where my family had no resources for fancy chemicals and so practised what would be called today "organic farming." Our trees, bushes and fields yielded wonderful foods, always changing with the seasons. My mother and grandmother took great care in turning these foods into delicious, simple meals. We strolled around the nearby forests gathering wild berries, wild mushrooms and fruits. My grandfather, in particular, taught me a great deal about using wild herbs in making medicinal oils and pastes from the flowers, seeds and roots. I was always attracted to food and, instead of playing soccer, I enjoyed helping my mom make sausages or preserves. Once a week I would get up early and make sourdough bread with her before I went to school. And so it seemed very natural that some years later I would serve as an apprentice in a commercial kitchen.

On first coming to Canada, I could not believe the abundance of "wild" food in western Canada. Years later, when I came to work for the owners of Canadian Rocky Mountain Resorts, Pat and Connie O'Connor, it seemed natural to pair the offerings of the setting with the cuisine. Early pioneers of this concept were mountain guides from Europe, particularly from Switzerland, who came with the builders of the national railway. They combined local foods with European culinary traditions and Rocky Mountain Cuisine was born.

Another pioneer of Rocky Mountain foods is certainly my long-time friend Walter von Rotz. He understands the harmony of pairing local ingredients with old-world cooking methods and giving each dish a contemporary flair. It was his venison smokies and air-dried buffalo, together with other delicacies, that made me come up with the original Game Platter, one of the favourites on our menu. I added my recipe for preserved mustard melons and Ken Canavan, the chef from our Cilantro restaurant, came up with an excellent sun-dried cherry relish. Full-fledged Rocky Mountain Cuisine had arrived!

Rocky Mountain Cuisine is a unique blend of contemporary cooking styles, using as many seasonal ingredients from the Canadian northwest as possible and preparing them in a healthy way. I encourage our young chefs not to follow fashions but to find harmony in foods. I use all natural ingredients in my cooking and never allow artificial colouring or flavourings because I do not think we need them. There is very little fat and cream in our recipes, but where they are used, they are used sensibly. Good food and food that is good can co-exist.

I love cooking and it gives me great pleasure in preparing food to make people happy. The *Rocky Mountain Cuisine Cookbook* contains recipes that reflect my interpretation of Rocky Mountain Cuisine. Some are very special and others are more simple, though no less tasty. Whether you are planning a festive dinner or just want to make some cookies, I hope these recipes provide as much joy to the cook as the guests.

The possibility that these recipes are something completely new under the blue Rocky Mountain sky is very slim, considering the number of recipes already published. But I honestly regard these recipes as those I developed over the years, cooking and living in the Rockies, as well as those handed down to me by my mother. Some are the results of working with talented staff and accepting their ideas; these are so noted.

If you have any comments, questions, complaints or suggestions, I would welcome a note. I much prefer letters to telephone calls because it's hard to devote sufficient time to callers when coping with three full lodges, two restaurants, a bakery, a staff crisis and elk feeding on my chives.

Please write to: Hubert Aumeier
                  Box 1598
                  Banff, Alberta
                  Canada
                  T0L 0C0

Thank you.

HUBERT AUMEIER
BANFF, ALBERTA
OCTOBER 1996

SOUPS

Fresh Pea Soup

SERVES 4

4 lbs	fresh peas
3	large russet or baking potatoes
6 cups	chicken stock (see page 70)
6	green onions
	Salt to taste
	Freshly ground white pepper
¼ cup	chopped chives

1. Shell the peas to produce 4 cups. Peel and coarsely chop the potatoes.
2. In a medium saucepan bring chicken stock to boil over medium-high heat.
3. Add potatoes to stock, reduce heat to medium-low, and cook until tender, about 10 minutes.
4. Chop the white parts only of the green onions, add to the stock and cook for 5 minutes.
5. Add peas, increase heat to medium, and cook for about 5 minutes, until peas are just tender. Do not overcook.
6. Purée the soup in a blender or food processor, then pass it through a strainer, pressing the mixture with a spoon.
7. Briefly reheat the soup, season with salt, freshly ground white pepper and chopped chives.

Red Pepper Corn Potato Chowder

SERVES 6 TO 8

1 lb	small red potatoes
1	medium white onion
4	sweet red peppers
3 tbsp	olive oil
8 cups	chicken stock (see page 70)
1 tsp	salt
1 tsp	freshly ground black pepper
1 tsp	dried thyme or 1 sprig fresh thyme
¾ tsp	blackening spice (see page 85)
1 cup	whipping cream
2½ cups	fresh or frozen corn kernels
	Fresh thyme for garnish

1. Peel and dice the potatoes into large cubes. Coarsely chop the onion and red peppers.

2. Heat oil in a large Dutch oven, add vegetables and sauté over medium heat until vegetables are softened, about 10 minutes.

3. Add stock and seasonings and bring to a boil. Cover, reduce heat and simmer for 45 minutes or until vegetables are completely cooked.

4. Remove from heat. Purée the soup in a blender or pass it through a food mill.

5. Return puréed mixture to Dutch oven and stir in cream and corn. Heat gently over medium heat until corn is warmed thoroughly. Garnish with fresh thyme.

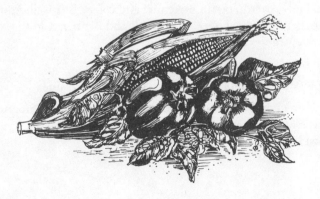

Leek and Salmon Chowder

SERVES 4

1	large leek
1	medium onion
1	carrot
3	large potatoes
1	fennel bulb (anise)
1	stalk celery
3 tbsp	vegetable oil
3 tbsp	unsalted butter
¾ cup	dry white wine
4 cups	fish stock (see page 72)
	Salt and pepper to taste
4 oz	black or regular smoked cod
1 cup	whipping cream
	Oil for deep-frying
½ lb	salmon fillet

1. Wash leek thoroughly, remove outer leaves and trim off wilted ends. Cut off about 4 inches of the green part and cut into fine strips. Rinse again and pat dry. Set aside for garnish. Dice the remaining part of the leek into small pea-size pieces.

2. Dice the onion into pea-size pieces.

3. Peel carrot and potatoes and clean fennel and celery. Dice into pea-size pieces.

4. In a large pot heat the oil, add butter and sauté onion until it begins to brown on the edges. Add leek, carrot, potatoes, fennel and celery. Stir well. Add white wine and fish stock, reduce heat, season with salt and pepper. Add the cod and simmer until the vegetables are cooked.

5. Remove cod and break it up into flakes.

6. Remove about half of the vegetables from the soup and set aside.

7. In a blender or with a hand-held mixer purée the soup. Stir in cream. Adjust seasonings if necessary. Return the soup to the pot and put back the vegetables which were set aside.

8. Cut the salmon into 1-inch cubes and add to the soup. Bring the soup back to the boil. The salmon will cook in the hot soup.

9. Deep-fry the strips of leek in hot oil, drain on paper towels and salt lightly. Do them in two or three batches.

10. Place flakes of cod on each plate, then ladle chowder, arranging the vegetables and pieces of salmon high in the centre.

11. Garnish soup with deep-fried leeks.

Roasted Butternut Squash Soup

SERVES 6 TO 8

2	medium butternut squash
1	medium sweet potato
1	large yellow onion
3 tbsp	unsalted butter
8 cups	chicken stock (see page 70)
	Salt and pepper to taste
2 tbsp	chopped fresh thyme

1. Preheat oven to 375°F.

2. Cut squash in half, remove seeds and place skin side up on a cookie sheet lined with parchment paper. Brush lightly with butter and roast in oven for about 1 hour or until squash is soft to the touch and the skin is browned. Scoop out the pulp and set aside.

3. Chop the sweet potato and onion into medium-size pieces. In a large pot melt the butter and sauté the onion and sweet potato. When the onion begins to glisten, add chicken stock and the squash. Cook until the potatoes are tender.

4. Purée the soup in a blender and return to heat. If soup is too thick, add a little more chicken stock. Season with salt, pepper and fresh thyme.

Wild Mushroom Soup

If possible, use a variety of dried wild mushrooms, such as porcini, chanterelles, morels, puffballs, lobster mushrooms or pine mushrooms.

SERVES 6 TO 8

2 cups	dried wild mushrooms
1½ cups	warm water
3 tbsp	unsalted butter
1	small white turnip, peeled and diced
1	medium yellow onion, diced
3	medium potatoes, peeled and chopped
6	cloves garlic, finely diced
1	leek, white part only
¼ cup	dry sherry
3	sprigs parsley
1	sprig fresh thyme
1	large bay leaf
3	juniper berries
8 cups	chicken stock (see page 70)
1 cup	whipping cream
	Salt and pepper to taste

SERVING SUGGESTION
Serve with thick slices of warm, grilled bread.

1. Place dried mushrooms in a bowl and cover with warm water. Allow to soften for 20 minutes. Strain soaking liquid through a sieve lined with a paper towel. Reserve the liquid. Rinse mushrooms thoroughly and cut into strips.

2. Melt butter in large Dutch oven over medium-high heat. Add turnip, onion, potatoes, garlic and leek. Sauté until golden, stirring frequently to avoid burning.

3. Add sherry and stir to deglaze the pan.

4. Wrap the parsley, thyme and bay leaf in a small piece of cheesecloth to form a bouquet garni.

5. Add bouquet garni and juniper berries, mushrooms, chicken stock and mushroom liquid to the pot and bring to a rolling boil. Immediately lower heat to medium and cook until liquid has been reduced by one-third. (Dip the handle of a wooden spoon into the mixture and note the level. Make a second mark on the spoon a third of the way down. When the mixture hits that level, you'll know it has been reduced by a third.)

6. Add the cream, bring soup to a boil, then remove immediately from heat. Allow to cool, then purée in a blender. Season to taste and reheat gently.

STARTERS

Chanterelle Mushroom Tartar with Pepper Duck

Start preparations for this dish one day before you plan to serve it. The duck must be marinated for 24 hours before being smoked. Stove-top smokers are available in specialty cookware stores.

If you prefer, you can buy smoked pepper duck or goose breasts and prepare just the chanterelle mushroom tartar.

SERVES 4

2	large duck breasts (about 1½ lb each)
¼ cup	salt
⅓ cup	loosely packed brown sugar
3 cups	water
1 cup	apple juice
2	cloves garlic, crushed
1	stalk celery
1	sprig fresh rosemary
3 tbsp	freshly cracked black peppercorns
½ lb	fresh chanterelle mushrooms
2 tbsp	unsalted butter
	Salt and pepper to taste
2 tbsp	herb vinegar
⅓ cup	finely chopped chives
1	ripe tomato, peeled, seeded and diced
	Whole chives for garnish

SERVING SUGGESTION
Serve with fresh rye bread, butter and radishes.

1. Trim duck breasts and cut off any loose fat. Score the covering of fat with crosswise strokes of a sharp knife.

2. Mix together salt, brown sugar, water, apple juice, garlic, celery and rosemary. Marinate the duck for 24 hours.

3. Remove the duck from the brine and pat dry. Press the meat side into a layer of crushed peppercorns.

4. Place on a smoking rack, fat side down, and smoke over hot smoke for 15 to 20 minutes or until done. Remove and set aside.

5. Clean the mushrooms with a sharp knife and rinse quickly. Sauté the mushrooms in the butter and season with salt and pepper. When juices begin to form in the pan, remove the mushrooms and chop into pea-size pieces.

6. Reduce the liquid to a few tablespoons and season with vinegar, or to taste. Return mushrooms to pan and add chopped chives and diced tomatoes and set aside. Mixture will be very thick.

7. Cut the duck breasts into thin slices and arrange in a circular pattern on plates.

8. Using two soup spoons or an ice-cream scoop, place a scoop of mushroom tartar in the centre of each plate. Garnish with whole chives and cracked black pepper.

Salmon Trout Salad with Belgian Endive and Potato Chips

SERVES 4

¼ cup	crème fraîche (see page 85)
2 – 4 tbsp	grated fresh horseradish
	Salt and pepper to taste
4	small Belgian endives
½	lemon
6 tbsp	clarified unsalted butter
4	4-oz salmon trout fillets (or salmon fillets)
½	bunch Italian flat leaf parsley
¼ cup	chives, cut in ½-inch pieces

1. Blend the crème fraîche with the horseradish and season with salt and freshly ground pepper. Set aside.

2. Wash endives and remove any wilted leaves. With a sharp knife cut out the stalks and chop the endives into finger-thick pieces. Season with salt, freshly ground pepper and the juice of ½ lemon.

3. Heat 2 tbsp of the clarified butter in a skillet and quickly sauté endive for one minute. It should not be wilted.

4. Season the trout with salt and freshly ground pepper. Heat the remaining 4 tbsp of clarified butter in a large frying pan and sauté the trout over medium heat for about 45 seconds on each side.

5. Remove to warm plates and drizzle with the crème fraîche sauce. Place a mound of potato chips in the centre of each fillet and sprinkle with chives chopped into ½-inch pieces.

6. Toss endives with the parsley and place beside the trout fillets.

POTATO CHIPS

4	large redskin potatoes
½ cup	melted unsalted butter

1. Preheat oven to 400°F.
2. Peel potatoes and cut lengthwise into thin slices (about the thickness of a toothpick). Keep sliced potatoes in water.
3. Pat potato slices dry and brush both sides with melted butter.
4. Place on baking trays lined with parchment paper, sprinkle with a little salt and bake for 6 to 10 minutes. Turn over the slices frequently, and as they begin to take on a light golden colour, brush with a little more butter.
5. When the potatoes turn a rich golden color, remove them from the oven and place on a tray lined with paper towels to soak up any excess butter.
6. These potato chips can also be served as appetizers with smoked salmon spread or as snacks.

Smoked Trout with Onion Marmalade

The preparation of the trout takes at least 1½ days and the juniper oil needs to be made 2 to 3 weeks in advance.

SERVES 4

FOR TROUT

1 cup	flavourless vegetable oil
¾ cup	crushed juniper berries
1½ cups	pickling salt
½ cup	loosely packed brown sugar
4 quarts	cold water
½	leek, white part only
1	medium onion
1	stalk celery
4	cloves garlic, crushed
5	bay leaves
¾ cup	fresh dill
2 tbsp	crushed white peppercorns
3 tbsp	yellow mustard seeds
4	whole trout (10 – 12 oz each)

SERVING SUGGESTION
This goes especially well with grated fresh horseradish and new potatoes.

FOR MARMALADE

6	large yellow onions
5	shallots
3 tbsp	vegetable oil
2 tbsp	honey
3 tbsp	raspberry vinegar
2 tbsp	red wine vinegar
½ cup	Merlot wine
	Salt and freshly ground black pepper to taste

1. In a clear glass bottle or jar combine flavourless vegetable oil with crushed juniper berries. Cover jar or bottle with a lid or cork and place it on a sunny window sill for 2 to 3 weeks. Strain off the berries and reserve oil.

2. In a ceramic crock dissolve salt and sugar in cold water.

3. Dice leek, onion and celery and wrap in cheesecloth along with the garlic, bay leaves, dill, peppercorns and mustard seeds. Hang the bag in the brine.

4. Clean the fish but do not remove bones. Soak in brine for at least 12 hours but not more than 24.

5. Remove the fish from the brine and dry it on a smoking rack. This will give the fish a sheen and will also seal in the protein and juices.

6. Smoke the fish over warm smoke (not hot and not over 75°F, for at least 24 hours. The smoking should not be interrupted, and the fire must be fed continuously. I like to add twigs of juniper to the sawdust).

7. Cool the fish, wrap in waxed paper and keep in a cool dry place.

8. To make the marmalade, slice the onions and shallots into very thin rings, using a mandolin.

9. In a large pot, preferably non-stick or enamelled, heat the vegetable oil and add the onions and shallots. When onions start to brown, reduce heat to lowest setting and continue browning. Stir occasionally.

10. When the onions are evenly dark brown, add the honey, raspberry vinegar, red wine vinegar, wine, salt and pepper. Increase the heat a little and reduce until onions take on a sheen and become caramelized.

11. Once all liquids are absorbed, adjust seasoning, if necessary, and transfer to a serving bowl or jar.

12. Remove skin and bones from trout. Place fillets, with the skinned side up, on a plate and brush gently with juniper oil. Heat for 1 minute under broiler.

13. Serve with onion marmalade.

Wild Mushroom Terrine with Pumpkin and Nasturtiums

SERVES 4

1 lb	mixed fresh wild mushrooms or oyster, shiitake, enoki or button mushrooms
2 tbsp	olive oil
2	shallots, chopped
2 tbsp	chopped fresh chervil
1 tbsp	chopped chives
	Salt and pepper to taste
4	gelatin leaves, soaked in cold water, or 1 envelope of gelatin
1 cup	cooked fresh pumpkin or cooked sweet potatoes
2 tbsp	crème fraîche (see page 85)
½	lemon
1	pinch ground nutmeg
1	handful nasturtium blossoms
1	handful small spinach leaves, young dandelion or wild strawberry leaves
2 tbsp	nut oil (e.g. walnut or hazelnut)

1. Clean mushrooms; only if necessary, wash under running water. Dry thoroughly and slice not too thinly.

2. Heat olive oil and sauté shallots until they become translucent. Add mushrooms and cook about 8 minutes. Season with chervil, chives, salt and pepper.

3. Squeeze gelatin leaves to remove excess water. Remove mushrooms from heat and stir in the gelatin leaves until gelatin is melted. If you are using an envelope of gelatin, place ¼ cup of water in a small saucepan and sprinkle in gelatin. Allow it to rest for 5 minutes, then heat gently to dissolve gelatin. Remove mushrooms from heat and stir in gelatin mixture.

4. Line a small terrine or loaf pan with plastic wrap and fill with mushroom mixture. Refrigerate for 6 hours.

5. In a blender purée the pumpkin with the crème fraîche and the juice from the lemon. Season with nutmeg, salt and pepper. Spoon pumpkin purée onto cold plates and top with a slice of mushroom terrine.

6. Toss nasturtium blossoms and leaves in nut oil and garnish the plates.

Ravioli with Lentils and Dandelion Sauce

SERVES 4

1 cup	French green lentils
4 tbsp	unsalted butter
3	cloves garlic, finely chopped
3	shallots, finely chopped
1 tbsp	finely chopped capers
1	lemon
2 cups	chicken stock (see page 70)
⅓ cup	blanched finely chopped spinach
⅔ cup	ricotta or cream cheese
1 tbsp	goat cheese
4 tbsp	grated Parmesan cheese (preferably Parmigiano-Reggiano)
	Salt and pepper to taste
¼ lb	dandelion leaves or frisée
¼ cup	chicken stock (see page 70)
½ cup	crème fraîche (see page 85)
1	package won ton wrappers

1. Soak lentils for 1 hour in cold water. Drain and set aside.

2. Melt 2 tbsp of the butter in a saucepan and sauté 2 cloves of finely chopped garlic and 2 finely chopped shallots until translucent. Add the lentils, capers, grated zest of the lemon and chicken stock. Cook over medium heat until tender, about 25 minutes. Set aside.

3. To make filling, combine spinach, ricotta, goat cheese, Parmesan and one clove of finely chopped garlic. Season carefully with salt and pepper. Set aside.

4. Wash the dandelion leaves and reserve a few tips for use later. Chop leaves finely. Melt remaining 2 tbsp of butter in a pan and sauté the leaves with 1 finely chopped shallot until wilted. Add chicken stock and reduce by half. Add crème fraîche and reduce again by half. Strain the sauce and season with salt and pepper.

5. Spoon filling onto won ton wrappers. Wet the edges with a little water and pinch together. Blanch the ravioli in boiling salted water.

6. Warm the lentils and spoon into the centre of deep plates. Place ravioli on top and drizzle with sauce which has been reheated. Add some tips of dandelion leaves to sauce at the very end.

Wild Boar Pâté

Prepare this pâté at least 48 hours before you plan to serve it.

SERVES 6

2	large chicken breasts, boneless and skinless
¾ lb	wild boar and/or pork (shoulder is best)
¾ lb	back fat from pork chops
½ cup	duck livers (optional, but great when used)
1	Granny Smith apple, peeled and cored
1½ tsp	salt
½ tsp	freshly ground black pepper
¼ tsp	ground nutmeg
3	juniper berries
4	bay leaves
1 tsp	mixed dried herbs – marjoram, sage, thyme
¼ cup	brandy
¼ cup	Port or Madeira
1 lb	bacon, preferably double-smoked
2	large eggs

SERVING SUGGESTION

Some good accompaniments to this pâté would be mustard melons (see page 80), figs, rye bread, radishes or pickled vegetables.

1. Dice the chicken, wild boar or pork, the fat and livers (if using) into walnut-size pieces.

2. In a very hot skillet quickly sauté the meat in small batches to brown on all sides. The meat should still be rare.

3. In a bowl place the meat and apple cut into chunks and sprinkle with salt, pepper, nutmeg, juniper, 1 bay leaf, dried herbs, brandy and Port. Mix well and cover. Chill for 24 hours.

4. Preheat oven to 400°F.

5. Remove the bay leaf and lift meat out of marinade, reserving liquid. Grind the marinated meat and apple in a meat grinder fitted with a coarse blade or in a food processor. Process in very small batches.

6. Dice the bacon into small pieces and mix into the pâté. Mix in the eggs and juices from the marinade and mix well. Spoon off about a tablespoon of pâté, form it into a small patty and fry it to test the seasoning. Adjust seasoning if necessary.

7. Fill a terrine or loaf pan with the meat, smooth the top and decorate with bay leaves. Bake in oven for 60 minutes.

8. While the pâté bakes, some fat will rise to the top. If you let the fat cool with the pâté, it will seal the meat and allow the flavours to develop more fully. Leave it for two days or so and you will be amply rewarded. The fat may be removed before serving, or may be eaten with the pâté, depending on preference. This pâté will keep chilled for six to eight days.

SALADS

Kohlrabi, Green Bean and Morel Salad

If fresh morels are not available, use fresh shiitake mushrooms instead.

SERVES 4

2 – 3	small, young kohlrabi
½ lb	young green beans
1	head butter leaf lettuce
¼ cup	fresh morels
1	shallot
1 tbsp	unsalted butter
¼ cup	extra-virgin olive oil
3 tbsp	sherry vinegar
	Salt and pepper to taste
¼ cup	chopped fresh chervil
¼ cup	chopped chives

1. Peel kohlrabi and cut into matchstick-size pieces.
2. Cut green beans into matchstick lengths and blanch in boiling salted water. They should still be crisp. Drain and immerse quickly in cold water. Drain again and set aside.
3. Clean lettuce. Wash morels and cut lengthwise into strips.
4. Mince the shallot and sauté in butter until translucent. Add morels and sauté for a few seconds more. Season with salt.
5. To make dressing, whisk together olive oil and sherry vinegar. Add salt and pepper to taste.
6. Toss kohlrabi, beans and morels with dressing.
7. Arrange lettuce leaves on plates and place a portion of salad on each. Sprinkle with chervil and chives.

Fireweed Shoots with Tomato Vinaigrette

The fireweed plant is not just pretty to look at but quite useful. The young leaves, when dried, make a beverage resembling black tea. The shoots can be served as a vegetable and the cotton-like seed pods can be used as filling for soft toys. The plant is also an excellent source for honey bees.

The shoots are a little sweet and taste like asparagus. You can substitute asparagus in this recipe if you are not able to find fireweed shoots to dig up.

SERVES 4

8 – 12	sheets of phyllo pastry
⅓ cup	melted unsalted butter
¼ cup	sesame seeds
1½ lb	fireweed shoots or green asparagus
3	ripe tomatoes
1	small red onion
¼ cup	chopped chives
	Salt and pepper to taste
4 tbsp	pumpkin seed oil (or 1½ tbsp hazelnut oil and 2½ tbsp olive oil)
2 tbsp	herb vinegar

1. Preheat oven to 350°F.
2. Layer four sheets of phyllo pastry, one on top of another and brush the top of the fourth sheet with melted butter. Place four more sheets on top and brush last sheet with butter. Sprinkle top with sesame seeds and cut into long triangles.
3. Bake in oven until crisp and golden, 10 to 12 minutes.
4. Clean shoots and wash thoroughly.
5. In a pot of boiling salted water blanch shoots until al dente. Drain and immerse shoots in ice water to retain bright colour.
6. Peel, seed and dice tomatoes. Finely dice onion and combine with chopped chives, salt and pepper, pumpkin seed oil and vinegar. Add mixture to tomatoes.
7. Place a bundle of shoots on each plate and top with tomatoes. Garnish with phyllo pastry triangles.

Snow Peas with Sweetbreads and Smoked Salmon

SERVES 4

1 lb	veal sweetbreads
5 cups	chicken stock (see page 70)
1 lb	young snow peas
4 tbsp	unsalted butter
1 tbsp	finely diced leek, white part only
1 tbsp	finely diced carrot
1 tbsp	finely diced fennel bulb (anise)
1 tbsp	finely diced celery
1	shallot, chopped
1 tbsp	kirsch
2	tomatoes
1	sprig fresh tarragon
¼ cup	dry white wine
¼ cup	whipping cream
1	pinch cayenne pepper
1 tbsp	cider vinegar
12	slices smoked salmon

1. Place sweetbreads in a bowl, cover with cold water and soak for at least 5 hours, to remove any remaining juices.
2. Drain and simmer sweetbreads in stock for 10 to 12 minutes.
3. Drain again and immerse quickly in ice water. Lift out carefully and without damaging the sweetbreads, remove the outer skin with a sharp paring knife.
4. Wrap sweetbreads in plastic wrap, place between two plates and weight it down for 2 hours in the refrigerator.
5. Remove strings from snow peas. Cook snow peas in boiling salted water and lift out while they are still crunchy. Set aside.
6. Melt 2 tbsp of the butter in a skillet and sauté the leek, carrots, fennel and celery. Add shallots and sauté without browning. Add kirsch.

7. Peel, seed and dice the tomatoes and add to the sautéed vegetables along with tarragon. Deglaze with white wine and a bit of water. Simmer for 10 minutes.

8. Strain the mixture, reserving the liquid. Discard the pulp and add cream to the liquid. Heat and reduce to about ¼ cup and season with cayenne pepper and cider vinegar.

9. Slice sweetbreads (about the thickness of a pencil), pat dry and season with salt and pepper. In a skillet, melt remaining 2 tbsp of butter and sauté sweetbreads until nicely browned on both sides.

10. Arrange snow peas on each plate, garnish with smoked salmon and warm sweetbreads. Drizzle with sauce and serve at once.

FISH AND SEAFOOD

Arctic Char with Snow Crab

This recipe from David Forestell is an entrée for special occasions. Salmon fillets can be substituted for arctic char.

SERVES 6

1 cup	each of diced potatoes, carrots, parsnip, turnip and rutabaga
3 tbsp	melted unsalted butter
½ cup	Italian flat-leaf parsley (whole leaves)
	Salt and pepper to taste
3 tbsp	unsalted butter
1 cup	chopped shallots
4	sprigs fresh thyme
5	cloves garlic, minced
2 cups	dry white wine (e.g. Sauvignon Blanc)
2 cups	whipping cream
6	6-oz arctic char fillets (or salmon fillets)
4 oz	fresh snow crab meat
2 oz	whitefish (or Sevruga) caviar (optional)
½ cup	chopped chives

1. Blanch the potatoes, carrots, celery, parsnip, turnip and rutabaga in boiling water until al dente. Drain and toss with 3 tbsp melted butter, parsley and salt and pepper to taste. Set aside.

2. To prepare sauce, melt 1 tbsp of the butter in a skillet over medium-high heat. Add shallots, thyme and garlic and sauté until golden, stirring constantly.

3. Add white wine and stir to deglaze pan. Stir mixture over high heat until almost all of the liquid has evaporated.

4. Add cream and continue cooking until mixture is reduced to about 3 cups. Strain sauce.

5. Preheat oven to 450°F.

6. Top each piece of fish with ½ tbsp of butter and season with salt and pepper. Place in oven for 6 to 8 minutes; do not overcook. Fish is done when firm to the touch but is still moist and flakes easily.

7. Gently reheat the vegetables.

8. Reheat the sauce and warm the flaked crab meat in it. Just before serving, spoon in the caviar.

9. To serve, place a portion of vegetables on each plate, top with a fillet of fish, spoon sauce over all.

Cod Fillets in a Potato Crust with Wild Mushrooms and Merlot Ragout

SERVES 4

2 cups	Merlot wine
1 cup	fish stock (see page 72)
¼ cup	Port
2 cups	assorted fresh wild mushrooms (e.g. chanterelle, bolete, trumpet, lobster, shiitake, pine) (approx. 8 oz)
2 tbsp	olive oil
4 tbsp	cold unsalted butter
4	large shallots, finely diced
2 – 3	large Idaho potatoes
4	8-oz cod fillets (or other white-fleshed fish, such as halibut, sablefish, turbot)
2 tbsp	chopped fresh thyme
	Salt and pepper to taste
1	egg white
4 tbsp	clarified unsalted butter
2	ripe tomatoes, peeled, seeded and diced or 1 cup small cherry tomatoes
	Sprigs of fresh thyme for garnish

1. Reduce the Merlot to ¾ cup. Add fish stock and Port and reduce further to ½ cup. Season with salt and pepper and set aside.

2. Clean the mushrooms by wiping carefully and leave as many as possible whole. Cut others into bite-size pieces. Sauté shallots in 2 tbsp of the cold butter and olive oil, add mushrooms and cook on medium heat until tender. Season with salt and pepper and set aside.

3. Wash and peel potatoes and julienne them, using a mandolin. Squeeze out any excess water and mix well with thyme, salt and pepper and set aside.

4. Season the fish with salt and pepper and dredge one side with lightly beaten egg white and coat with the potato. Press firmly. With the potato side down, fry 2 pieces of fish in 1½ tbsp of the clarified butter in a non-stick pan until the potatoes are golden. Turn fish over and cook other side. Fry the remaining 2 pieces of fish in 1½ tbsp of clarified butter.

5. Sauté tomatoes in remaining 1 tbsp of clarified butter.

6. Bring the Merlot sauce to a boil and whisk in the remaining 2 tbsp of cold butter quickly.

7. To serve, place a portion of mushroom ragout on each plate, along with the fish, potato crust facing up. Pour the sauce around the fish and mushrooms and garnish with sautéed tomato and sprigs of thyme.

Big Rock Porter Mussels

SERVES 4

3 lb	mussels
2 tbsp	olive oil
2	cloves garlic, cut in half
½ cup	julienned double-smoked bacon
2	shallots, finely diced
1	carrot, finely diced
1	leek, white part only, finely diced
2	stalks celery, finely diced
	Salt and freshly ground black pepper to taste
1	bottle Big Rock porter beer
1 cup	warm fish stock (see page 72)
½ cup	chopped parsley
⅓ cup	chopped chives

SERVING SUGGESTION
I like to serve fresh grilled white sourdough bread and more porter with this dish.

1. Clean the mussels thoroughly and discard any broken ones.

2. In a large shallow pot heat olive oil and brown garlic. Discard garlic. Add bacon, stir, and add shallots, carrot, leek, and celery and sauté briefly over high heat.

3. Add mussels, season with a little salt, stir in the beer and the fish stock. Cover with a tight-fitting lid and cook over high heat until mussels open.

4. Remove mussels to a large platter and check for any unopened ones. *Discard all unopened mussels.*

5. Reduce remaining stock by one-half and add parsley and chives. Season with freshly ground pepper. Pour sauce over the mussels and serve immediately.

Salmon Carpaccio with Asparagus

SERVES 4

1½ lb	salmon fillet, preferably cut from back loin
1½ cups	mixture of finely chopped fresh herbs – basil, Italian parsley and thyme
2 tbsp	crushed black peppercorns
½ cup	Pinot Noir
⅔ cup	olive oil
	Salt and pepper to taste
1	bunch green onions
1 lb	green asparagus
2 tbsp	olive oil
1 tbsp	chopped shallots
2	cloves garlic, finely chopped
¼ cup	dry white wine
¼ cup	water
1	large bay leaf
2 – 3 tbsp	vegetable oil
	Parsley or fresh basil for garnish

SERVING SUGGESTION
A fresh baguette and a Pinot Noir go well with this dish.

1. Cut the salmon into strips about 1" wide, 1" thick and 6" long. Sprinkle the finely chopped basil and parsley onto a baking sheet. Rub the crushed pepper into the salmon, roll in the herbs and refrigerate for 2 to 3 hours.

2. Heat the Pinot Noir in a small saucepan and reduce by three-quarters. Let cool slightly. Put into a blender and incorporate ⅓ cup of olive oil in a light stream at high speed. Season to taste with salt and pepper. Remove and set aside mixture.

3. Clean blender. Clean and blanch green onions and purée in blender. Add ⅓ cup of olive oil in a light stream and emulsify at high speed. Season with salt.

4. The salmon and the oils may be prepared one day in advance.

5. Wash the asparagus thoroughly and snap off the ends. With a vegetable peeler, peel the stem.

6. In a wide skillet, heat 2 tbsp of the olive oil, sauté the shallots and garlic. Add asparagus. Add wine, water and bay leaf. Cover and let the asparagus braise for about 4 to 6 minutes (depending on size of stalks). Remove from stock, let cool but do not refrigerate.

7. Heat vegetable oil in a heavy skillet, preferably cast iron, and quickly sear the salmon over high heat. Cook about ½ minute on each side, for a total of 2 minutes. Remove from pan and cool immediately in refrigerator.

8. To serve, slice the salmon and arrange in an attractive pattern on the plates. Add asparagus spears, drizzle with the oils and garnish with fresh parsley or basil.

Salmon with Wild Rice Cannelloni

I like to use wild rice pasta, but this dish works just as well with other pasta such as whole wheat, poppy seed, hazelnut and dill, etc.

SERVES 4

2	large sweet red peppers
1	large yellow pepper
2 tbsp	diced onion
2 tbsp	olive oil
2 tbsp	diced leek, white part only
2	cloves garlic, minced
1	small sprig fresh thyme
2 cups	fish stock (see page 72) or white vegetable stock (see page 71)
2 tbsp	dry sherry
2 tbsp	sun-dried tomatoes, not packed in oil
4	sheets fresh wild rice pasta (or other flavour), about 6 x 6 inches each
1½ lb	spinach
2 tbsp	butter
3 tbsp	chopped fresh basil
3 tbsp	chopped fresh thyme
	Few needles of fresh rosemary
4 tbsp	crumbled goat cheese
4	6-oz salmon fillets
	Salt and pepper to taste
	Sprigs of fresh thyme for garnish

1. On a charcoal grill or over a gas burner roast the red and yellow peppers until they are charred and blistered. Transfer them to a bowl and cover with plastic wrap; the condensation will help loosen the skin. When the peppers are cool, peel off the skin.

2. Cut off the tops and bottoms from the peppers and remove seeds. From the remaining portions, cut small diamond shapes and reserve for garnish. Save the trimmings for use later.

3. Sauté the diced onion in olive oil until it is translucent but not browned. Add leek, one clove of garlic, a little of the thyme and the red and yellow pepper trimmings and continue sautéeing briefly.

4. Deglaze the pan with fish stock and sherry and add rest of the thyme. Simmer for 35 minutes or until the mixture is reduced by one-half. Strain and press through a fine mesh sieve, extracting as much liquid as possible. Reserve juices to make pepper essence and discard pulp.

4. Put sun-dried tomatoes in a small bowl and pour hot water over them. Let sit for 10-15 minutes. Drain and cut tomatoes into fine strips.

5. In a large pot of boiling water, blanch the pasta. Rinse in cold water and pat dry.

6. Thoroughly wash spinach and blanch in boiling water. Squeeze well. You should have about 2 cups of cooked spinach. Loosen the leaves.

7. Sauté remaining clove of garlic in butter and add spinach, season with salt and pepper and toss in the sun-dried tomatoes. Set aside.

8. Lay out the sheets of pasta and sprinkle each with basil, thyme and rosemary. Add spinach and crumbled goat cheese on top. Roll up pasta to form cannelloni. Place in ovenproof dish.

9. Preheat oven to 400°F.

10. In a heavy ovenproof skillet sear the salmon over high heat. Turn the fish over and place in the oven for 6 to 8 minutes. The salmon should be medium-rare.

11. At the same time, bake the cannelloni, lightly buttered and covered, in the oven for 10 minutes, or heated through.

12. Heat pepper essence and add pepper diamonds.

13. Cut each cannelloni in half and place the pieces in a large deep soup plate. Place the salmon on the cannelloni, set off slightly to form a contrast. Ladle 2 to 3 tbsp of essence around the salmon. Serve the rest on the side. Garnish with a sprig of thyme.

Orange-Infused Salmon with Fiddleheads and Pecan Wild Rice

SERVES 4

4 cups	fresh fiddleheads (or frozen)
1 cup	wild rice
4	sprigs fresh thyme
2	oranges
1 cup	pecan halves, toasted
1	bunch green onions
4	6-oz salmon fillets (skin on)
1 tbsp	vegetable oil
2	lemons
¼ cup	unsalted butter
	Salt and white pepper to taste
	Sprigs of fresh thyme for garnish

1. If using fresh fiddleheads, wash, soak and rinse them several times until there is no dirt in the rinse water. Set aside.

2. In a pot, place rice and 2 cups of water and 1 sprig of thyme. Bring to a boil and continue boiling for 45 minutes, uncovered. Reduce heat to low and continue cooking for 1 hour. The rice is ready when the grains start to split open, but still have a little bite to them. Don't worry if all the grains are not split. Drain off any remaining water, remove the thyme and set aside.

3. Preheat oven to 350°F.

4. Segment the oranges by first peeling off the skin with a paring knife, removing all the white parts as well. Holding the orange over a bowl, cut each segment away from the skin. Squeeze the juice from the remaining core, then discard core. Set aside the orange segments and the juice.

5. Place the salmon fillets in a ceramic or glass ovenproof dish and season with salt and pepper. Place orange segments and juice on and around the salmon, sprinkle salmon lightly with vegetable oil. Bake for 10 minutes.

6. Place the fiddleheads in a pot of lightly salted boiling water and cook until they turn bright green and are almost cooked through. Drain and set aside.

7. Grate the zest of the lemons and squeeze out juice. Set aside.

8. In a large sauté pan combine the cooked wild rice, 3 sprigs of thyme which have been chopped, lemon juice and zest, green onions, pecans and butter. Toss the ingredients over high heat, then add the fiddleheads. Season with salt and pepper to taste.

9. To serve, place one quarter of the rice mixture on each plate, place a piece of salmon on top and drizzle any juice from the salmon over top. Garnish with a sprig of thyme.

Trout with Lentil-Zinfandel Sauce

SERVES 4

1	small onion, finely chopped
4 tbsp	unsalted butter
1¼ cups	diced double-smoked bacon
1	bouquet garni (2 sprigs parsley, 1 sprig fresh thyme, 1 large bay leaf, tied in a bundle)
1 cup	brown lentils
2 cups	Zinfandel wine
1 cup	brown veal stock (see page 68)
	Salt and pepper to taste
4	8-oz trout fillets
3 tbsp	herb vinegar

SERVING SUGGESTION
A mixture of diced carrots, parsnips, beets, leeks, small onions and baby potatoes, either steamed or sautéed with some diced double-smoked bacon, goes especially well with this dish.

1. Sauté the onion in 1 tbsp of the butter until golden. Add the diced bacon and bouquet garni. Add lentils, wine and veal stock. Bring to a boil and season with salt and pepper. Skim off any foam.

2. Simmer for 30 to 45 minutes. Cook slowly so that lentils do not lose their shape. Lentils are cooked when they have softened but still hold their shape.

3. Season the trout with salt and pepper and sauté in 1 tbsp of butter in a skillet until crisp but medium-rare. Remove fish and deglaze pan with herb vinegar. Swirl in 2 tbsp of butter until melted.

4. Place a portion of lentils on each plate, top with trout fillet and drizzle with pan juices.

MEAT AND GAME

Pronghorn Antelope Chops
with Corn Cakes and Elderberry Sauce

Antelope is plentiful in the foothills of the Rockies. Although not commonly served in restaurants, the meat is very tasty because the animal feeds on grasses and grains. Venison or lamb chops can be substituted, if antelope is not available.

SERVES 4

3 lbs	pronghorn antelope or venison or lamb chops
½ tsp	crushed juniper berries
2 tbsp	olive oil
1	large egg
3 – 4 tbsp	flour
2 tbsp	milk
2 tbsp	whipping cream
¾ cup	fresh or frozen corn kernels
	Salt and freshly ground pepper to taste
2 tbsp	vegetable oil
¼ cup	Madeira
1 tbsp	Cognac
⅓ cup	game stock (see page 69)
2 – 3	elderberries or blueberries or 1 tbsp elderberry jam
2 tbsp	unsalted butter
4	grilled small leeks and/or grilled whole pine mushroom caps (or shiitake mushroom caps)

1. Clean off the antelope chops and scrape down the bones.

2. Marinate the chops with juniper berries and olive oil for 2 hours.

3. In a bowl beat the egg and whisk in flour. Whisk in milk and cream. Set aside to allow batter to rest for 30 minutes.

4. Add corn to the batter and cook small pancakes in a non-stick pan. Keep warm.

5. Season antelope with salt and freshly ground pepper. Put the vegetable oil in a pan and heat. Sear chops quickly on both sides and reduce heat. Finish cooking to medium rare or as desired. Keep warm.

6. Scoop off any fat from the pan and deglaze with the Madeira and Cognac. Add game stock and reduce by one-half.

7. Strain the sauce and add berries (or jam). Bring sauce to a boil, turn off heat and whisk in butter.

8. Arrange corn cakes and antelope chops on plates, with grilled leeks and/or grilled whole pine mushroom caps. Drizzle chops with sauce and serve at once.

Seared Beef Tenderloin

SERVES 4 AS AN APPETIZER

12 oz	beef tenderloin (whole piece)
3 tbsp	vegetable oil
¾ tsp	salt
2 tsp	freshly ground black pepper
¾ – 1 tsp	blackening spices (see page 85)
2 tsp	Worcestershire sauce
¼ cup	sun-dried cherry relish (see page 79)

1. Rub beef with a mixture of 2 tbsp of the oil, salt, pepper and blackening spices.

2. Heat remaining oil in frying pan or broiler pan and sear meat on one side, about 4 minutes. Turn meat over, brush with Worcestershire sauce and continue cooking, 3 to 5 minutes, depending how you like your beef cooked.

3. Remove from heat and allow to rest approximately 5 minutes. Slice into 12 equal portions.

4. Arrange 3 slices per plate and top meat with 1 tbsp of sun-dried cherry relish.

Lamb Carpaccio in Hot Vegetable Vinaigrette

SERVES 4

1	large carrot
1	leek, white part only
1	fennel bulb (anise) or 1 cup sugar peas
1	medium onion
1	small celery root (celeriac)
¾ cup	olive oil
	Salt and cracked black pepper to taste
1	sprig fresh rosemary
3 – 4 tbsp	balsamic vinegar
2	8- to 10-oz lamb loins
½ cup	julienned fresh mint and thyme
	Watercress for garnish

1. Dice the carrot, leek, fennel, onion and celery root into small pieces.
2. Heat olive oil and add the diced vegetables, salt and cracked black pepper, and rosemary and simmer until the vegetables are al dente. Pour the hot oil and vegetables over the lamb loins and marinate for 4 to 5 hours. (If you prefer, you can sear the lamb — medium-rare — before marinating.)
3. Remove lamb from marinade and pat dry. Strain off the vegetables and set aside.
4. Cut the lamb lengthwise into very fine slices and arrange on plates.
5. Toss the vegetables with balsamic vinegar, a few julienned mint leaves and thyme leaves. Adjust seasoning.
6. To serve, place a scoop of vegetables on the lamb and garnish with watercress.

Grilled Lamb Sausages with Cumin

MAKES 8 SMALL SAUSAGES OR PATTIES

1 lb	boneless lamb shoulder
1 lb	boneless pork shoulder
2	cloves garlic, peeled and minced
5 tsp	salt (or to taste)
2 tsp	freshly ground pepper
1 tsp	granulated sugar
¾ tsp	ground cumin
5 tbsp	chopped Italian flat-leaf parsley
3 – 4 tbsp	ice water
1 cup	finely diced roasted red pepper
	Sausage casings (lamb or pork) (optional)

SERVING SUGGESTION
Serve with new potato salad or over pasta.

1. Cut the lamb and pork into 1-inch cubes and chill for 3 hours. Pass the meat through grinder fitted with a medium to large disk (about ¼-inch holes).

2. In a large bowl combine the meat with the garlic, salt and pepper, sugar, cumin, parsley, ice water and roasted peppers. Mix quickly, preferably with your hands.

3. Use a sausage stuffer to fill sausage casings. If you prefer, you can make patties.

4. Prick each sausage with a needle and grill them over medium heat for about 8 to 10 minutes.

Alberta Lamb Chops with Glass Noodles and Mint-Lavender Vinaigrette

SERVES 4

2	Alberta racks of lamb, frenched (16 to 18 oz each)
1 cup	vegetable oil
4	cloves garlic, chopped
½ cup	chopped fresh mint
1 tbsp	Dijon mustard
1 tsp	freshly ground pepper
1	package dried rice vermicelli
½ cup	rice wine vinegar
1½ cups	extra-virgin olive oil
	Salt and freshly ground pepper to taste
	Handful edible lavender flowers or chive flowers
	Handful fresh chives
1 cup	cherry tomatoes
½	sweet red pepper
½	yellow pepper
4	Sprigs of fresh mint and lavender or chive flowers for garnish

1. If your rack of lamb is not frenched, clean the fat off the bones down to the eye of the lamb.

2. Combine vegetable oil, garlic, ¼ cup of chopped mint, mustard and freshly ground pepper in a shallow dish and marinate the lamb in the refrigerator overnight. Lamb should marinate a full 24 hours.

3. Soak the rice noodles in enough boiling water to cover. When noodles are soft (about 5 minutes), drain off water and set aside.

4. To make dressing, mix the vinegar and olive oil in a bowl. Season with salt and pepper to taste. Add remaining ¼ cup of chopped mint to the vinaigrette. Don't use a whisk. Stir in some lavender flowers. Set dressing aside.

5. Cut the chives into 1- to 2-inch pieces. Set aside. Quarter the cherry tomatoes and set aside.

6. Remove the tops and bottoms of the peppers and save for future use. Cut each pepper in half lengthwise and cut into very thin strips. Mix the two colours of peppers together and set aside.

7. Heat the barbecue grill to medium-high.

8. Remove the lamb from the marinade and drain well. Place lamb on the grill and cook to medium-rare (or to preference).

9. While the lamb is cooking, toss the noodles with the vinaigrette, chives, peppers and tomatoes.

10. Cut the racks of lamb into individual chops.

11. Arrange some noodle salad in the centre of each plate and on each side of the salad, place a lamb chop with the bone facing in and up. Lean the two chops against one another. Garnish with a sprig of mint and lavender or chive flowers.

Pork Tenderloin with Rhubarb Chutney Stuffing and Mashed Potatoes

SERVES 4

FOR RHUBARB CHUTNEY:

1 cup	granulated sugar
½ cup	orange juice
1	orange
¾ cup	Merlot wine
1½ cups	fresh or frozen cranberries
1 cup	fresh or frozen chopped rhubarb
1	stick cinnamon
1½ tsp	cracked black pepper
1 tbsp	chopped fresh ginger

FOR TENDERLOIN:

1	leek, white part only
8	shiitake mushroom caps
1	shallot
2 tbsp	unsalted butter
	Salt and pepper to taste
½ cup	whipping cream
2 lb	pork tenderloin
2 tbsp	chopped fresh marjoram
2 tbsp	vegetable oil
½ cup	brown stock (see page 68)

FOR MASHED POTATOES:

4	large Idaho potatoes
1	large celery root (celeriac)
1 cup	hot milk
3 tbsp	unsalted butter
1	pinch ground nutmeg
	Celery leaves for garnish

1. Melt sugar until it is a golden caramel colour. Deglaze pan with orange juice and continue cooking until sugar is dissolved. Grate the zest of one orange and add to pan along with red wine, cranberries, rhubarb, cinnamon, black pepper and fresh ginger.

2. Simmer 20 to 30 minutes, until mixture reaches the consistency of jam, but the fruit still has some chunks in it.

3. Skim off foam from top, remove cinnamon stick and pour into sterilized jars. The chutney may be prepared a week in advance. This recipe makes 1⅔ cups, more than you need here, but the flavour improves with time and you can keep it for future use.

4. Clean leek thoroughly and dice finely. Clean mushrooms and dice finely. Finely dice shallot and sauté in 2 tbsp of butter. Add leeks and mushrooms, season with salt and pepper and add cream. Reduce over medium-high heat until vegetables are soft and cream is almost all absorbed. Cool and set aside.

5. Cut tenderloin into four portions, about 8 oz each. With the handle of a wooden spoon make a hole lengthwise in the tenderloin and stuff with leek mixture. Rub with fresh marjoram and set aside.

6. Peel potatoes and celery root and chop into large pieces. Boil until tender, then drain. Immediately mash potatoes and celery root with milk and 3 tbsp of butter. Season with salt, pepper and a pinch of nutmeg. Keep warm.

7. Preheat oven to 375°F.

8. Brown the tenderloins in 2 tbsp of oil in a skillet. Finish off the cooking in the oven, about 12 minutes per side, for 20 to 24 minutes.

9. Remove meat and keep warm. Deglaze the roasting pan with the brown stock. Reduce stock, strain and reserve.

10. On each plate place a scoop of mashed potatoes shaped in the form of a cone. Slice each tenderloin into 5 to 6 slices and lean the slices against the cone. Drizzle sauce around the base of pork and spoon 4 to 5 small drops of chutney onto the sauce. Garnish with whole celery leaves.

Rabbit with Savoy Cabbage and Poppyseed Pasta

Although this recipe originally called for wild rabbit, we use domestically bred rabbit in our restaurant. Either pork tenderloin or chicken thighs can be substituted for rabbit, but why not give rabbit a try?

SERVES 4

FOR SAUCE:

1 lb	rabbit bones or chicken bones, chopped
3 tbsp	vegetable oil
1 cup	diced mixed leek, carrot, celery, onion
1 cup	Merlot or Cabernet wine
2 cups	water
6	juniper berries
1	sprig fresh rosemary
1	sprig fresh thyme
½ cup	rosehip jam
3 tbsp	unsalted butter
1 tbsp	crème fraîche (see page 85)

FOR RABBIT:

2	8-10 oz boneless saddles (loins) rabbit
	Salt and pepper to taste
4 tbsp	unsalted butter
1	Savoy cabbage
¾ lb	oyster mushrooms
2	shallots, finely chopped
¼ cup	finely chopped parsley
3	egg yolks
¼ cup	whipping cream

FOR PASTA:

¾ lb	penne pasta
3 tbsp	poppyseeds
¼ cup	unsalted butter or cold-pressed sunflower seed oil

1. Preheat oven to 375°F.

2. Roast the chopped bones in the oven with the oil until they are brown. Add the cup of diced mixed vegetables and continue roasting until everything is a dark caramel colour, but not burnt.

3. Deglaze pan with wine and water, add juniper berries, rosemary and thyme and reduce sauce to ½ cup. Strain.

4. The sauce can be prepared ahead of time to this stage and refrigerated.

5. Heat sauce with rosehip jam, 3 tbsp of butter and crème fraîche and keep warm.

6. Season rabbit with salt and pepper. Melt 2 tbsp of butter in a skillet and sauté fillets for about 30 seconds to seal in juices. Set aside to cool.

7. Loosen and remove 4 to 6 large cabbage leaves and cut away the hard veins. Blanch the leaves in boiling salted water for about 3 minutes, then immediately dip them in ice water. Dry off the leaves on paper towels and set aside.

8. Clean off mushrooms (if possible, do not wash) and dice coarsely. In a skillet melt 2 tbsp of the butter and sauté shallots over medium heat until golden. Add mushrooms and cook on high heat for 5 minutes. Add parsley and salt and pepper to taste.

9. Combine egg yolks with cream and add to the mushrooms. Bring to a boil and remove from heat. Cool.

10. On a sheet of plastic wrap place 2 or 3 cabbage leaves, overlapping them. Place half of the mushroom filling in centre and top with a fillet of rabbit. Roll up cabbage to form a tight log, using the plastic wrap to pull up the leaves. Twist ends of wrap like a candy wrapper. Repeat with remaining cabbage and rabbit.

11. Preheat oven to 400°F.

12. Remove plastic wrap and place cabbage rolls on a parchment-lined baking sheet. You can tie the rolls with string, if you like. If you can get pork caul, it is ideal for wrapping the cabbage in place of the plastic wrap. The pork dissolves when cooked. You can also wrap the cabbage rolls in foil, with the ends twisted like a candy wrapper.

13. Bake in oven for 25 minutes. Remove and let meat rest for 5 minutes before slicing into 1-inch pieces. If you have used foil, let the meat rest in the foil.

14. Cook pasta until al dente and drain well.

15. In an ungreased skillet (not non-stick) toast the poppyseeds for several minutes. Remove and grind finely in a mortar (or a clean coffee grinder set aside for spices).

16. Toss the hot pasta in butter or sunflower seed oil and poppyseeds. Gently heat mushroom sauce.

17. Place pasta on plates and arrange slices of cabbage roll against the pasta. Spoon sauce around pasta and cabbage.

Venison Medallions with Orange-Ginger Glaze and Sun-Dried Cranberries

SERVES 4

1½ lb	rack of venison
⅓ cup	vegetable oil
10	juniper berries, cracked and toasted
20	black peppercorns, cracked
1 tsp	minced garlic
1 tsp	chopped fresh sage
1 tsp	chopped fresh basil
2 tbsp	salt
1 tsp	ground white pepper
1 tsp	paprika
1 tsp	ground ginger
¾ cup	orange juice, freshly squeezed
¾ cup	brown stock (see page 68)
2 tsp	minced fresh ginger
2 tsp	brandy
⅓ cup	dry white wine
½ cup	orange marmalade (not too bitter)
¼ cup	sun-dried cranberries (see page 86)
1	pinch salt
1 tbsp	chopped Italian flat-leaf parsley

SERVING SUGGESTION
I like this dish served over Fennel and Potato Gratin with Goat Cheese (see page 61). Fresh beans are a good accompaniment.

1. Clean venison of all silver skin and tendon and clean bones (or have your butcher do this).
2. Combine oil, juniper berries, peppercorns, garlic, sage, basil and ¼ cup of the orange marmalade and marinate venison in this mixture for 12 to 24 hours.
3. Remove meat from marinade; save marinade. Season meat with salt, white pepper, paprika and ginger.
4. Preheat oven to 375°F.
5. In a greased ovenproof pan on high heat sear the meat on all sides, then place in the oven. For tender meat, cook medium or medium-rare, about 20 to 30 minutes. Baste with the marinade every 7 to 8 minutes, but do not baste for the last 10 minutes.

6. While meat is in the oven, prepare the sauce. Soak cranberries in hot water for 5 minutes. Drain and set aside. Combine orange juice, brown stock, ginger, brandy and wine and reduce by one-half. Add remaining ¼ cup of marmalade, one-half of the cranberries and salt. Adjust seasoning. Garnish with parsley and rest of the cranberries.

7. Carve rack and serve, with sauce on the side.

Venison Carpaccio with Chanterelle Tartar

SERVES 4

1 tbsp	dry mustard powder
4 – 5 tbsp	apple juice
	Salt and crushed black pepper to taste
1 cup	fresh chanterelle mushrooms
2	shallots, diced
1 tbsp	olive oil
⅓ cup	chopped chives (not green onions)
2 tbsp	balsamic vinegar
3 tbsp	extra-virgin olive oil
	Salt and freshly ground black pepper
12 oz	venison loin
	Sun-dried cherry relish for garnish (see page 79)

1. Mix together mustard powder, apple juice, salt and crushed pepper until smooth. Set aside.

2. Clean chanterelles and quickly sauté with shallots in olive oil for 1 to 2 minutes. Remove from heat and allow to cool.

3. Dice the chanterelles, add to chopped chives and season them with vinegar and extra-virgin olive oil. Add salt and pepper to taste. Tartar will be quite stiff.

4. Slice venison into 12 pieces and season with salt and pepper. In a very hot skillet sear the venison until brown on each side, about 30 seconds per side. The meat should be rare to medium-rare. Remove from pan and brush lightly on one side with mustard mixture.

5. With a small cup or ladle place a scoop of mushroom tartar on each plate. Place 3 slices of venison around the tartar and garnish with cherry relish.

Venison Sirloin with Vegetables and Port Reduction

When preparing this dish, be sure to allow enough time to marinate the venison for 4 to 6 hours or even overnight.

SERVES 4

6	cloves garlic, crushed
1 tbsp	chili flakes
1 tbsp	ground cinnamon
2 tbsp	vegetable oil
4	6-oz venison loins
2 – 3	large leaves Savoy cabbage
¼ cup	finely diced carrots
¼ cup	finely diced parsnips
¼ cup	finely diced celery root (celeriac)
¼ cup	finely diced Yukon Gold potatoes
6 oz	double-smoked bacon
¼ cup	granulated sugar
½ cup	Port
1 tbsp	balsamic vinegar
1 cup	game stock (see page 69)
1	sprig fresh rosemary
2	juniper berries
1	bay leaf
	Salt and pepper to taste
½ cup	sun-dried cherries (see page 86)
2	large sweet potatoes
	Oil for deep frying
1 tbsp	olive oil
1 tbsp	butter
¼ cup	finely diced fresh chanterelles or other wild mushrooms
	Sprigs of fresh rosemary for garnish

1. Mix together the garlic, chili, cinnamon and vegetable oil and marinate venison in mixture for 4 to 6 hours or overnight.

2. Remove from marinade and pat dry. Set aside.

3. Wash cabbage leaves and cut into 1-inch strips. In boiling salted water blanch carrots, parsnips, celery root, potatoes and cabbage until tender. Drain and set aside.

4. Cut bacon into 1-inch long, pencil-like strips. In boiling salted water blanch bacon for about 3 minutes. Drain, set aside to cool.

5. In a stainless steel pot melt sugar until golden caramel in colour. Deglaze with Port and vinegar. Over medium-high heat reduce by one-half. Add stock, 1 sprig of rosemary, juniper berries and bay leaf and reduce again by one-half. Season with salt and pepper.

6. Soak the cherries in hot water for 5 minutes. Drain and add to the stock. Keep warm.

7. Slice the sweet potatoes very thinly, using a mandolin, and deep fry in hot oil until crisp. Drain on paper towel and keep warm.

8. In a hot skillet sear venison for 3 minutes on each side for medium-rare. Set aside.

8. Heat the olive oil and butter in the skillet and toss the blanched vegetables, bacon and mushrooms until hot. Season with salt and freshly ground pepper.

9. To serve, spoon vegetables in a mound in the centre of deep plates. Slice each loin into 4 pieces and arrange them in a circle over the vegetables. Drizzle sauce at base of meat, making sure not to cover up the natural colour of meat. Serve remainder of sauce on side. Sprinkle with sweet potato chips and garnish with sprigs of rosemary.

Braised Venison with Bread Muffins and Winter Vegetables

SERVES 4

4	venison shanks (or 8 if small) or lamb shanks
1	small leek, white part only
1	carrot
2	stalks celery
1	onion, cut into two pieces
1	sprig fresh thyme
1	bay leaf
	Salt and pepper to taste
¼ cup	all-purpose flour
4 tbsp	vegetable oil
4 tbsp	tomato paste
4 cloves	garlic, minced
1 tsp	dried marjoram
2 cups	game stock (see page 69) or brown stock (see page 68)
¼ cup	each of root vegetables – e.g. carrot, turnip, celery root, acorn squash, parsnip, small onions, Savoy cabbage, Brussels sprouts

1. Prepare each shank by removing the meat around the end of the bone and scraping the bone clean.

2. Wash leek, carrot, celery, and onion halves and tie together, along with thyme and bay leaf to form a bundle.

3. Season meat with salt and pepper and dust with flour. Heat oil in a heavy roasting pan and brown on all sides. Add the bundle of vegetables to the roasting pan.

4. Preheat oven to 450°F.

5. Place meat, uncovered, in oven for 20 minutes. Turn the meat over and remove fat. Mix together tomato paste, garlic, marjoram and stock and add to pan.

6. Reduce heat to 375°F and braise shanks until tender, for 45 minutes or more. Turn them frequently.

7. Wash and dice your choice of root vegetables into large pieces. Blanch in boiling salted water until al dente. Drain and reserve.

8. Check the shanks and remove from oven if done. Skim off grease from roasting pan and reduce liquid to ½ cup. Season with salt and pepper to taste.

9. In a skillet melt the remaining 2 tbsp of butter and stir-fry the diced vegetables, 6 to 8 minutes. The vegetables should still be crunchy.

10. Arrange vegetables in deep pasta dishes, set shanks on top and garnish with muffins (recipe below). Drizzle sauce over all and/or serve on the side.

BREAD MUFFINS

2 cups	stale rye bread
6 tbsp	unsalted butter
2 tbsp	diced double-smoked bacon
1 tbsp	finely diced onion
1 tbsp	chopped pecans
2 tbsp	ground hazelnuts
2	large eggs
1	pinch ground nutmeg
⅓ cup	warm milk

1. To prepare muffins, cut bread in small cubes and sauté in 3 tbsp of the butter.

2. Fry the bacon and discard fat. Sauté onion in 1 tbsp of the butter.

3. In a large bowl mix together the bread, pecans, hazelnuts, bacon, onions, eggs and nutmeg. Pour in the warm milk.

4. Knead mixture well and scoop into 4 buttered ramekins or a muffin tin. Place ramekins in a baking pan filled with hot water reaching halfway up the sides of ramekins. Put into oven in which the shanks are cooking and poach for about 20 minutes. Remove from oven and turn out the muffins.

POULTRY

Quails Stuffed with Figs and Wild Rice

I prefer to use quails with the bones in, because I think they taste better when roasted on the bone and also look more attractive. However, the recipe works just as well with boneless quails tied up with string.

SERVES 4

8	quails
1	lemon
1	orange
4	cloves garlic, minced
4 tbsp	chopped Italian flat-leaf parsley
	Salt and freshly ground pepper
4 tbsp	canola oil
2 tbsp	Chinese soya sauce
1	bag black tea
8 – 10	dried figs
1 cup	cooked wild rice, well drained
½ tsp	chopped fresh mint
½ tsp	fennel seeds, toasted
2 tbsp	coarsely chopped pecans
⅓ cup	Port
2 tbsp	vegetable oil

1. Clean quails inside and out and pat dry.
2. Remove zest and juice of lemon and orange and combine with garlic, 2 tbsp of the parsley, salt and pepper, canola oil and soya sauce to make a marinade.
3. Baste quails with marinade and place them in a ceramic dish. Pour marinade into dish and chill for at least 6 hours or, better still, overnight.
4. Prepare one cup of strong black tea and soak figs in tea until soft. The tea removes sulfides. Cut each fig into quarters and halve each quarter.
5. In a large bowl combine cooked rice, the remaining 2 tbsp of parsley, mint, fennel seeds, pecans, Port and salt and pepper and mix well.

6. Remove quails from marinade and drain well. Stuff the quails with rice mixture and close openings with toothpicks. Season quails lightly with salt and pepper. Discard marinade.

7. Preheat oven to 375°F.

8. In a roasting pan or large ovenproof skillet (preferably cast iron) heat oil and quickly sear the breasts, one or two at a time. Return quails to pan and bake in the oven for 20 to 25 minutes. Baste occasionally with cooking juices. Remove from oven and keep warm for about 5 minutes to allow juices to settle.

9. Serve with drippings.

Chicken Apple Sausages

MAKES ABOUT 12 SMALL SAUSAGES OR 4 PATTIES

3 lb	boneless skinless chicken breast or leg
3 tbsp	salt
	Freshly ground white pepper to taste
3	cloves garlic, finely diced
1 tbsp	chopped fresh thyme
2 tbsp	unsalted butter
1	medium onion, finely diced
2	tart apples (e.g. Granny Smith or Boskoop), peeled and finely diced
2 – 3 tbsp	loosely packed brown sugar
	Sausage casings (lamb or pork) (optional)

1. Ask your butcher to coarsely grind the chicken. Thoroughly mix the ground chicken with salt, freshly ground pepper, garlic and thyme. Chill for 45 minutes.

2. Melt butter in a skillet over medium-high heat and sauté onion until soft and translucent. Add the apples and brown sugar and sauté on high heat until the apples take on some colour, but do not overcook. Chill for two hours.

3. Combine chicken and apples and with a sausage stuffer, fill the sausage casings. If you prefer, you can make them into patties. Prick each sausage with a needle and either sauté them in a frying pan or grill them until browned and cooked through, about 10 minutes.

Duck with Winter Spices

SERVES 4

½ cup	pitted prunes
¼ cup	dark rum
¼ cup	hot water
2	oranges
3	tart apples (e.g. Granny Smith or Boskoop)
1 tbsp	lemon juice
1	5 – 6 lb duck
½ cup	ice water
⅓ cup	duck stock (see page 69) or chicken stock (see page 70)
1	pinch cayenne pepper
½ tsp	gingerbread spice (see page 84)
	Salt and pepper to taste
¾ cup	Merlot or Zinfandel wine
¼ cup	brandy
2 tbsp	unsalted butter (optional)

1. In a bowl cover the prunes in rum and water. Grate the zest of ½ orange and add to prunes.

2. Peel the oranges and cut into segments, removing membrane. Peel apples, cut into quarters and remove cores. Add oranges, apples and lemon juice to prunes, mix well and place in refrigerator for 3 hours.

3. Drain the fruit, reserving the juices. Stuff duck with fruit and sew up.

4. Preheat oven to 400°F.

5. Place duck in roasting pan, drizzle with ice water and roast until crispy, about 1 hour. Baste with water every so often in order to produce crispy skin.

6. While the duck is roasting, reduce the reserved fruit juices to a syrup in a saucepan. Add dark stock, reduce again and season with cayenne pepper, gingerbread spice and salt and pepper to taste.

7. Remove the duck from the oven and keep warm. Skim off grease from roasting pan, add wine and brandy and deglaze pan. Strain into the fruit sauce. Add butter if you wish.

8. Place a scoop of fruit stuffing on each plate and arrange slices of duck in an attractive pattern. Pour sauce over meat.

Lacquered Game Hens

SERVES 4

4	Cornish game hens
2 tbsp	olive oil
	Salt and pepper to taste
6	slices rye bread
3 tbsp	unsalted butter
2 tbsp	shallots, finely chopped
1 lb	zucchini, finely chopped or grated
2	fresh apricots, diced
1	egg
2	sprigs fresh marjoram, chopped
2 tbsp	white vermouth
1 tbsp	cream cheese, softened (optional)
¼ cup	dark beer
2 tbsp	dark honey or fir-needle honey (see page 73)
2 tbsp	apricot jam
1 tsp	tomato paste
1 tbsp	sherry vinegar

1. With kitchen shears, starting at the neck, cut open the game hen along the backbone. Flatten hens, skin side up. Starting at the neck, with your fingers loosen the skin from the breast meat. Season both sides of meat with salt and pepper. Brush skin lightly with olive oil.

2. Remove the crusts from bread, cut into cubes and sauté in 2 tbsp of the butter. Sauté shallots in 1 tbsp of butter.

3. Combine bread, shallots, zucchini, apricots, egg, marjoram, vermouth, cream cheese and salt and pepper to make stuffing. Fill the pockets under the skin with stuffing.

4. Make a slit near the end of the breast and insert the leg bone through it to give the bird some shape. Place on a baking sheet.

5. Preheat oven to 375°F.

6. Combine beer, honey, jam, tomato paste and vinegar and mix well. Brush this lacquer over the skin of the hens.

7. Roast hens for 25-30 minutes, or until juices run clear. Baste occasionally with remaining lacquer. If the skin is browning too quickly, cover with foil.

Guinea Fowl in "Birch Bark"

The recipe originally called for birch bark which imparted a subtle flavour to the fowl and added an impact to the presentation of this dish. However, these days we are much more conscious of the damage we inflict on the ecology, and so we try not to destroy trees unnecessarily. If you can obtain birch bark in an ecologically sound way, do try the original recipe. Otherwise, use foil. This recipe also works well with chicken, game hens or pheasant.

If using birch bark, soak 4 sheets, 6" x 8" each, in lightly sugared water overnight.

This recipe, using real birch bark, has been selected as a finalist at the original National Wild Game Cooking Competition in the U.S.

SERVES 4

4	guinea fowl
4	large thin slices of pork back fat
	Salt and pepper to taste
1½ lb	baking potatoes
1–1½ cups	all-purpose flour
1	large egg
1	egg yolk
¾ tsp	salt
2 tbsp	melted unsalted butter
2	carrots
1	leek, white part only
2	small onions
1	stalk celery
2 tbsp	olive oil
1	bay leaf
15	black peppercorns
¼ cup	dry red wine
¼ cup	Ruby Port
½ cup	game stock (see page 69) or chicken stock (see page 70)
3 tbsp	unsalted butter
	Salt and pepper to taste

1. Remove breasts of the guinea fowl and reserve legs for another use (they are tough). Finely chop the carcass.

2. Season breasts with salt and pepper and wrap in the pork fat.

3. Peel, chop and boil potatoes. Drain and let steam dissipate.

4. Preheat oven to 400°F.

5. Into a large bowl, squeeze potatoes through a ricer. Add flour, egg, egg yolk and salt to form a dough.

6. On a floured surface roll out the dough into a rectangle big enough to wrap the breasts. Wrap the breasts with dough and place each on a piece of foil or birch bark and bake in oven for about 20 minutes. If using birch bark, the packages will need to be tied with string.

7. Clean carrots, leek, onions and celery and chop coarsely.

8. In a skillet sauté carcasses in olive oil, along with the chopped vegetables, bay leaf and peppercorns. Add wine and Port and reduce to about ¼ cup. Deglaze with game stock and reduce a little more. Strain through a fine sieve. Whisk in butter and keep warm. Adjust seasoning if necessary.

9. If using birch bark, remove the string and place each opened package on a plate and deliver with a flourish to the table. Serve with sauce.

Roasted Pheasant with Quince and Walnuts

This recipe can be used with guinea fowl, snipe, quails or free-range chicken.
The birds should be seasoned with sage 24 hours before serving.

SERVES 4

2	small pheasant, 1½ lb each
4	fresh sage leaves
	Salt and pepper to taste
1 tbsp	unsalted butter, softened
2 tbsp	unsalted butter, cold
2	shallots, finely diced
4 tbsp	chopped walnuts
3 tbsp	quince jelly
½ cup	red wine
¼ cup	Port
¼ cup	chicken stock (see page 70)
2 cups	water
2 cups	white vinegar
2¼ cups	granulated sugar
3	quince
1 tbsp	finely chopped walnuts, lightly toasted
	Sprigs of fresh thyme for garnish

1. From the neck side of the bird, insert a fresh sage leaf under the skin of each breast. Let rest for 24 hours.

2. Preheat oven to 375°F.

3. Season birds with salt and pepper and roast in oven for 35 to 45 minutes or roast on a spit.

4. In a skillet, melt butter and sauté the shallots until transparent. Add 4 tbsp chopped walnuts and quince jelly and caramelize lightly. Add wine and Port and reduce to about ¼ cup. Add chicken stock and reduce a little more. Whisk in the cold butter and keep warm.

5. In a shallow pot combine the water, vinegar and sugar and mix well until sugar is dissolved. Place quince in this liquid and cook over high heat until quince is translucent and liquid thickens to the medium-syrup stage (about 225°F on a candy thermometer). The quince can be prepared up to 7 days in advance and stored in a sterilized jar in the refrigerator.

6. Slice the quince and, if you have prepared the quince in advance, heat lightly in a non-stick skillet or microwave oven.

7. Carve birds and serve over slices of quince. Sprinkle with walnuts and garnish with sprigs of thyme.

SIDE DISHES

Polenta with Pestos

These pesto recipes make more than is required in the polenta but the extra can be stored in the refrigerator for about a week.

SERVES 4 TO 6

FOR POLENTA

8 cups	chicken stock (see page 70)
1 tsp	salt
¼ tsp	ground black pepper
1 tsp	basil pesto
1	pinch ground nutmeg
2 cups	coarse cornmeal
1	large egg
¼ cup	grated Parmesan cheese (preferably Parmigiano-Reggiano)
½ cup	sun-dried tomato pesto
½ cup	basil pesto
1 tbsp	unsalted butter

FOR BASIL PESTO

2 cups	fresh basil
½ cup	pine nuts
1 tsp	salt
8	cloves garlic, peeled
½ cup	olive oil
½ cup	grated Parmesan cheese (preferably Parmigiano-Reggiano)

FOR SUN-DRIED TOMATO PESTO

1 cup	sun-dried tomatoes, not packed in oil
1 cup	olive oil
½ cup	chopped fresh basil
½ cup	grated Parmesan cheese (preferably Parmigiano-Reggiano)

1. In a large heavy pot bring chicken stock, salt, pepper, 1 tsp. basil pesto and nutmeg to a boil. Gradually add cornmeal in a fine stream, stirring continuously until all liquid is absorbed and polenta appears to be sticking to bottom of pot, 25 to 30 minutes. Remove from heat, wait for 2 to 3 minutes, then add egg and Parmesan cheese.

2. To make the tomato pesto, soak the sun-dried tomatoes in hot water, just to cover, for 5 minutes. Drain. Blend all the ingredients in a blender until smooth.

3. To make basil pesto, blend all the ingredients in a food processor until smooth but thick. Add more oil if necessary.

4. In a lightly oiled 8" x 12" baking dish, spread one-third of the polenta and smooth it out. Spread ½ cup of tomato pesto on top, then a layer of polenta, followed by a layer of basil pesto, then the remaining polenta.

5. Cover with plastic wrap and refrigerate overnight.

6. Remove from refrigerator and cut portions into squares or triangles. In a non-stick pan, fry in butter until golden.

Wild Mushrooms with Squash and Cranberries

When preparing mushrooms for this dish, use only the caps. Save the stems for use in stocks.

SERVES 4

1 lb	butternut squash
½ cup	dried morels
½ cup	dried porcini mushrooms
¼ cup	olive oil
2 tbsp	minced shallots
½ tsp	minced garlic (optional)
2 cups	sliced fresh shiitake mushrooms
2 cups	sliced fresh oyster mushrooms
1 cup	quartered fresh field mushrooms
1 tbsp	chopped fresh thyme
¼ cup	sun-dried cranberries (see page 86)
¼ cup	dry white wine (optional)
2 tbsp	unsalted butter
	Salt and freshly ground black pepper to taste

SERVING SUGGESTION
Serve hot with crusty bread.

1. Peel and seed squash. Slice into ribbons. Blanch squash in boiling water, drain and set aside.

2. Soak dried morels and porcini mushrooms in water for about 10 minutes. Drain and set aside.

3. Heat oil in pan and sauté shallots and garlic until translucent. Add all the mushrooms and sauté for about 10 minutes. Add thyme and cranberries and deglaze with wine. Season with salt and pepper and simmer for 1 to 3 minutes until tender.

4. In a separate pan heat butter and sauté blanched squash until hot. Season to taste with salt and pepper.

5. Place mushrooms in the centre of a portion of squash, making sure that the squash shows around it.

Fennel and Potato Gratin with Goat Cheese

SERVES 4

1	fennel bulb (anise)
2	large firm red-skinned potatoes
	Salt and pepper to taste
2 tbsp	melted unsalted butter
½ cup	beef stock (see page 66) or chicken stock (see page 68)
2 tbsp	fresh thyme leaves
4 oz	goat cheese

SERVING SUGGESTION
Serve this as a side dish with Venison Medallions with Orange-Ginger Glaze and Sun-Dried Cranberries (page 44).

1. Preheat oven to 375°F.

2. Clean fennel and remove stalk and any dirty leaves. Remove tough outer veins with a vegetable peeler. Cut the bulb in half, then into thin slices, about ⅛ inch thick.

3. Peel potatoes, wash and slice ⅛ inch thick. (If not using immediately, keep slices covered in water.) In a buttered ovenproof gratin dish or individual ramekins or cups (about 4" in diameter) arrange potatoes and fennel in alternating layers, finishing with layer of potatoes. Season each layer lightly with salt and pepper. Drizzle melted butter and stock over potatoes.

4. Bake, covered, in oven for approximately 25 minutes. Uncover, crumble goat cheese on top and sprinkle with thyme leaves. Bake, uncovered, for 20 minutes longer, or until potatoes are cooked.

5. To serve, cut into wedges. Leftover gratin can be reheated in the oven or a microwave oven.

Vegetarian Squash Cakes

For a very unusual variation, substitute young carrot greens for the peas.

SERVES 8

2 lb	butternut squash
¼ cup	unsalted butter
3 tbsp	chopped shallots
6	large eggs
¾ cup	whipping cream
½ cup	small broccoli florets
2 tbsp	chopped fresh dill
1 tsp	minced fresh ginger
1	pinch ground nutmeg
	Salt and pepper to taste
1 cup	brown vegetable stock (see page 71)
1 cup	fresh or frozen peas
½ cup	julienned fresh shiitake mushrooms
1 cup	flavourless vegetable oil
1 tsp	chopped fresh mint leaves

1. Peel and seed squash and dice into 1-inch cubes.
2. Melt butter in a saucepan and sauté shallots over medium heat until translucent. Add squash and stir. Add just enough water to cover the squash and cook over medium heat until soft and tender.
3. Drain off any remaining liquid (you may keep for sauce, if you wish) and let steam dissipate from squash.
4. With a food mill or in a food processor purée squash until very smooth. In a bowl combine eggs and ½ cup of the cream. Add the squash.
5. With a wooden spoon fold in broccoli, dill, ginger and nutmeg. Season with salt and pepper.
6. Preheat oven to 375°F.

7. Spoon into 8 well-buttered 4-oz ramekins. Place ramekins in a pan filled with 1 inch of hot water and bake in oven for 25 to 30 minutes.

8. While ramekins are in oven, bring vegetable stock to a boil in a pot. Add peas and cook until tender (for frozen peas cook about 2 to 3 minutes to retain nutrients and colour).

9. Transfer to a food processor and purée until smooth.

10. Strain the purée back into the pot and keep hot. Add remaining ¼ cup of cream (this is optional but sauce tastes much better with it). Season with salt and pepper.

11. Heat oil and quickly deep-fry shiitake mushroom strips in two batches until crisp. Drain on paper towels and sprinkle with salt. This garnish can be made in advance.

12. Add mint to sauce and ladle onto plates. Remove squash from ramekins and place on top of sauce. Sprinkle with mushrooms.

Wild Rice Waffles with Berry Butter

For the berry butter use a mixture of berries, two-thirds red and one-third dark. Strawberries, raspberries, blueberries, blackberries, red currants, black currants, gooseberries, cranberries — whatever is in season.

Prepare the butter at least one day in advance.

SERVES 4

½ cup	unsalted butter
1 cup	seasonal mixed berries
3 tbsp	icing sugar
2 cups	all-purpose flour
1 tbsp	baking powder
1 tsp	baking soda
½ cup	granulated sugar
½ cup	sour cream
4	large eggs, separated
½ cup	melted unsalted butter
1 cup	milk
1	pinch salt
¼ tsp	pure vanilla extract
1 cup	cooked wild rice, drained and dry
	Fresh mint leaves or strawberry blossoms for garnish

SERVING SUGGESTION
Pure maple syrup, on the side, can be served with these waffles.

1. Whip butter until fluffy and pale.

2. Set aside about ¼ cup of berries for garnish.

3. Mash berries coarsely with a fork, add 1 tbsp of the icing sugar and with a rubber spatula gradually work the berries into the butter. Don't worry if the mixture looks as though it is separating. Mix well and transfer into a serving dish.

4. Chill overnight or longer to allow flavours to develop.

5. In a bowl mix together flour, baking power, baking soda and granulated sugar. In a second bowl mix together sour cream, egg yolks, melted butter, milk, salt and vanilla.

6. Beat the egg whites until soft peaks form.

7. Combine the flour mixture and sour cream mixture and fold in egg whites. Fold in wild rice.

8. Bake waffles according to instructions accompanying your waffle iron.

9. Bring the berry butter to room temperature. With a spoon dipped in hot water, place one scoop of berry butter on each waffle. Sprinkle reserved berries on top and dust lightly with remaining icing sugar. Garnish with mint leaves or strawberry blossoms, if available.

Banana Pancakes

SERVES 4

1 cup	all-purpose flour
1 tbsp	granulated sugar
1 tsp	baking powder
½ tsp	baking soda
¼ tsp	salt
1¼ cups	buttermilk
1 tbsp	vegetable oil
½ tsp	pure vanilla extract
1	large egg
1½ cups	chopped ripe bananas
3 tbsp	chopped pecans, toasted

SERVING SUGGESTION
Serve with pure maple syrup.

1. In a large bowl combine flour, sugar, baking powder, baking soda and salt. Mix well.

2. In a small bowl combine buttermilk, oil, vanilla and egg and mix well. Add egg mixture to flour mixture and stir until smooth. Fold in bananas.

3. On a hot non-stick griddle or non-stick skillet spoon out ⅓ cup of batter for each pancake. When the surface is covered with bubbles and edges look cooked, turn over the pancakes. Continue cooking until done.

4. Sprinkle with pecans.

Pumpkin-Cornmeal Pancakes

SERVES 4

¾ cup	all-purpose flour
¾ cup	yellow cornmeal
¼ cup	firmly packed brown sugar
1 ½ tsp	baking powder
1 tsp	pumpkin pie spice
½ tsp	baking soda
½ tsp	salt
1⅔ cups	buttermilk
¾ cup	canned pumpkin
2 tbsp	vegetable oil
3	egg whites
2	egg yolks

SERVING SUGGESTION
A little fireweed or clover honey heated and served with the pancakes is also delicious.

1. In a large bowl combine flour, cornmeal, sugar, baking powder, spice, baking soda and salt and mix well.

2. In a smaller bowl combine buttermilk, pumpkin, oil, egg whites and egg yolks and mix well. Add egg mixture to flour mixture and stir until smooth.

3. On a hot non-stick griddle or non-stick skillet spoon out ⅓ cup of batter for each pancake. Cook for 1 minute on each side, or until done. (**Note:** bubbles will not form on top and edges will not look cooked.)

4. Serve with a syrup made of ¾ cup of fir-needle honey (see page 73) heated with 3 tbsp of water, or maple syrup, either plain or flavoured (see page 74).

STOCKS, CONDIMENTS AND JAMS

Basic Brown Stock

MAKES 1 CUP

2 lb	bones, veal or a mixture of equal parts of veal, pork and beef (ask your butcher to chop the bones into walnut-sized pieces)
2 – 3 tbsp	vegetable oil
1 cup	mixture of diced leek, celery, carrot, onion
1 tsp	tomato paste or 1 or 2 ripe tomatoes
1 cup	Merlot or Cabernet wine
6 cups	cold water
1	sprig each of fresh rosemary, fresh thyme and parsley
1	bay leaf
	Skins of 1 – 2 onions
1 tbsp	black peppercorns
	Salt to taste

1. Preheat oven to 450°F.
2. Place the chopped bones along with the oil in a pan and roast in the oven until browned, about 20 minutes. Remove from oven, drain off any fat, add tomato paste and return to oven.
3. Continue roasting until the bones are very dark. Stir frequently.
4. Add the diced vegetables and roast until mixture is dark but not burnt. Deglaze with the wine and 2 cups of water.
5. Add rosemary, thyme, parsley, bay leaf, onion skins, peppercorns and salt and when reduced to about ½ cup, remove from oven and place on stovetop. Add 4 more cups of water and simmer for 2 to 3 hours. Skim off any foam and fat from the top of the stock.
6. Strain stock and reduce again, down to 1 cup. Strain through a very fine sieve or cheesecloth and transfer to a storage jar, or freeze in ice cube trays. Transfer the frozen cubes into freezer bags.

Lamb Stock

Follow instructions for Basic Brown Stock but make the following substitutions:

- Use lamb bones and add ½ of a whole garlic bulb, crushed, when roasting the bones.
- Increase the rosemary to 2 sprigs.

Game Stock

Follow instructions for Basic Brown Stock but make the following substitutions:

- Use the bones of game.
- Add 6 to 7 juniper berries, ¼ cup dried mushrooms, ¼ cup Ruby Port in step 5.

NOTE
Dried mushrooms can be very expensive, so I save the stems of button mushrooms and shiitake mushrooms and dry them in the sun or the oven at 120°F. They can be used in sauces or stock.

Duck Stock

Follow instructions for Basic Brown Stock but make the following substitutions:

- Add one tart apple when roasting the vegetables in step 4.
- Add 2 bay leaves instead of 1 and add ½ sprig of fresh or ½ tsp of dried marjoram in step 5.

Chicken Stock

This stock is handy when you are making sauces or soups, or poaching poultry. If you use a boiling chicken, the meat can be used for salads or sandwiches.

MAKES 2 TO 3 CUPS

2 lbs	chicken or veal bones or 1 boiling chicken, cleaned (Ask your butcher to chop the bones into walnut-size pieces.)
2 cups	mixture of diced leek, white and light green parts, celery, onion, carrot
1 – 2	ripe tomatoes
1	sprig fresh thyme
1	sprig parsley
1	bay leaf
	Salt and pepper to taste

1. In a large pot bring water to a boil, add bones or chicken and bring back to a rolling boil for 2 minutes.

2. Drain off and rinse with cold water.

3. Return bones to pot and add 8 to 10 cups of cold water. Bring to a boil and skim off any foam. Add leeks, carrots, celery, onions and tomatoes and the thyme, parsley, bay leaf, salt and papper. Simmer gently for about 2 hours.

4. Remove bones and strain stock through a fine sieve or cheesecloth. For a more concentrated stock, reduce to 2 or 3 cups. Season to taste with salt and pepper.

5. Refrigerate the stock so that the fat can be skimmed off easily.

6. The stock can be frozen in an ice-cube tray and the frozen cubes transferred to a freezer bag. It provides a very convenient supply.

White Vegetable Stock

MAKES 6 TO 8 CUPS

1 cup	sliced white onion
1 cup	diced leek, white and light green parts
½ cup	diced celery
2 – 3 tbsp	corn oil
½ cup	diced carrots
½ cup	chopped very ripe tomatoes
¼ cup	chopped cauliflower
½ cup	chopped Savoy cabbage
4 – 5 tbsp	chopped parsley
1 tbsp	chopped fresh thyme
½ tsp	dill seeds
1	bay leaf
2	cloves garlic, crushed
2 tbsp	spiced olive oil
6	white peppercorns
	Salt to taste
8–10 cups	cold water

1. Sauté the onion, leek and celery in oil in a large pot until onion is translucent, about 6 to 7 minutes. Add carrots, tomatoes, cauliflower and cabbage and sauté for another 12 minutes, to bring out all the flavours. Make sure the vegetables do not brown.

2. Add the parsley, thyme, dill, bay leaf, garlic, spiced oil, peppercorns and salt, and fill the pot with 8 to 10 cups of water. Simmer for 35 to 40 minutes.

3. Strain stock through a fine mesh sieve or cheesecloth and adjust seasoning. For a more concentrated stock, reduce it further.

Brown Vegetable Stock

Follow the recipe for Basic Brown Stock, page 68, minus the bones.

Basic Fish Stock

A good fish stock depends on the quality of the ingredients. Use only very fresh bones and trimmings of white, preferably flat fish — e.g. halibut, sole, turbot. Salmon, which is too fatty, will not do.

MAKES 6 TO 8 CUPS

2 cups	finely chopped onion
2 tbsp	olive oil
2 cups	mixture of diced leeks (white and light green parts), celery root (celeriac), carrots
2 lb	bones and trimmings of white fish
8–10 cups	cold water
½ cup	dry white wine
1 tsp	cracked white peppercorns
2 – 3 tsp	chopped parsley
1 tsp	chopped fresh thyme
1 tsp	fresh dill
1	bay leaf
	Salt to taste

1. In a large pot sauté onions in olive oil until translucent. Do not let them brown. Add leeks, celery root and carrots and sauté for another 5 minutes.
2. Add fish bones and trimmings and sauté for a few minutes more.
3. Add cold water, wine, peppercorns, parsley, thyme, dill, bay leaf and salt and simmer for 20 minutes only. Do not simmer longer or you will extract the gelatin from the bones.
4. Strain the stock through a fine mesh sieve or cheesecloth and adjust seasoning.
5. If you wish a more concentrated stock, reduce it further.
6. Freeze stock for future use.

Fir-Needle Honey

This is a recipe I recall from my childhood. Each spring my grandmother, my mother, my brother and I used to go off into the woods to collect the first light green fir shoots. We were only allowed to pick a few from each tree in order to protect the growing cycle. Whenever I collect shoots here in the Rockies, I remember those days and maintain the same respect for the trees.

When making fir-needle honey, be sure to use only freshly gathered light green shoots which are a few days old and are still closed and firm. They should be about 1 inch long.

Makes 3 ½ cups

8–10 cups	fir shoots
¼ cup	fresh young raspberry leaves
¼ cup	clover blossoms
¼ cup	fresh mint leaves (wild, if available)
6	dandelion flowers (optional)
6 cups	loosely packed brown sugar or 2 cups maple syrup

1. Wash the fir shoots, raspberry leaves, clover blossoms and mint leaves.
2. In a large pot barely cover the fir shoots, raspberry leaves, clover blossoms, mint leaves and dandelion flowers with water.
3. Add sugar and bring to a boil. Reduce heat and simmer until the syrup thickens and becomes a rich brown in colour, about 3 to 4 hours. Test the consistency by dropping a spoonful onto a cold plate; it should form a soft ball.
4. Strain the syrup through a cheesecloth and further reduce to a thick syrup.
5. Place in sterile jars and cover with lids while honey is still hot.
6. If honey crystallizes, just place jar in warm water for a short time.

Flavoured Maple Syrups

BLUEBERRY MAPLE SYRUP

MAKES ABOUT 8 CUPS

2 cups	very ripe blueberries, fresh or frozen
1 cup	water
1	lemon
½ cup	corn syrup
1 quart	pure Canadian maple syrup

1. Clean blueberries and crush in a saucepan. Add water, juice of one lemon and corn syrup and simmer for 5 to 6 minutes.

2. Press through a fine mesh sieve, extracting as much liquid as possible with a rubber spatula.

3. Mix hot syrup with maple syrup and bring to a rolling boil. Reduce heat and simmer for another 5 to 6 minutes. Skim off any foam. Bottle in sterilized containers and let cool. Refrigerate.

4. To serve, reheat and add a few berries.

RASPBERRY MAPLE SYRUP

MAKES ABOUT 8 CUPS

2 cups	very ripe raspberries, fresh or frozen
1 cup	water
1	lemon
½ cup	corn syrup
1 quart	pure Canadian maple syrup
3 – 4 tsp	grenadine

1. Clean raspberries and crush in a saucepan. Add water, juice of one lemon and corn syrup and simmer for 5 to 6 minutes.

2. Press through a fine mesh sieve, extracting as much liquid as possible with a rubber spatula.

3. Mix hot syrup, maple syrup and grenadine (to improve the colour) and bring to a rolling boil. Be careful not to boil the syrup too long or it will turn a purplish colour. Reduce heat and simmer for another 5 to 6 minutes. Skim off any foam. Bottle in sterilized containers and let cool. Refrigerate.

4. To serve, reheat and add a few berries.

Flavoured Vinegars

Flavoured vinegars are too often misused, but in moderation they add a refreshing touch to dressings or condiments. Always use a very good quality vinegar, not the ordinary white vinegar commonly used for cleaning windows. Allow these vinegars to steep for about a week before using.

BLUEBERRY VINEGAR

MAKES 4 CUPS

1 lb	very ripe blueberries
4 – 5 tbsp	granulated sugar
3 cups	white wine vinegar

1. Bruise the berries, add sugar and a little water and bring to a boil.
2. Place the berries in vinegar in a ceramic container covered with a cloth and steep for four or five days at room temperature.
3. Strain through a cheesecloth and bring to a boil. Cool and place in sterilized bottles. Seal bottles with cork.

MAPLE HONEY VINEGAR

MAKES 5 CUPS

1 cup	flavourful honey
½ cup	maple syrup
4 cups	cider vinegar

1. Heat honey and maple syrup until honey is dissolved.
2. Add vinegar and simmer for 6 to 8 minutes.
3. Place in a ceramic container covered with a cloth and steep for one week at room temperature.
4. Strain and place in sterilized bottles.

BURNT-ORANGE AND ROSEMARY VINEGAR

MAKES 3½ CUPS

2	oranges
½ cup	granulated sugar
½ cup	water
4 cups	white wine vinegar
2 – 3	large sprigs fresh rosemary

1. Wash oranges and remove peel with a vegetable peeler. Cut peel into very fine strips.
2. In a small pot melt sugar to a light caramel colour and add orange peel.
3. Cook until orange is cooked and candied. Deglaze the pan with ½ cup of water.
4. Add vinegar and simmer for 6 to 8 minutes.
5. Chop rosemary and pour vinegar over it. Place in a ceramic container covered with a cloth and leave at room temperature for one week.
6. Strain and place in sterilized bottles.

Apple Cider Vinaigrette

MAKES 2 CUPS

1	Granny Smith apple
¼ cup	apple cider vinegar
¼ cup	sherry or champagne vinegar
⅛ cup	pure hazelnut oil
¾ cup	sunflower oil
2	shallots, minced

SERVING SUGGESTION
Use on mild-tasting leaves, such as butter leaf lettuce, also chicken salad or scallop salad.

1. Peel the apple and dice very finely.
2. Whisk together the vinegars and oils. Mix in apple and shallots.
3. Pour into sterilized bottles. Keeps for about one week in refrigerator.

Cherry Tomato Relish

This relish was created at Jasper Park Lodge by my friend Philippe Derrien, who was Grill Room chef at the time.

   Use tomatoes grown outdoors; they are more flavourful than hothouse ones.

MAKES 5 TO 6 CUPS

4 lbs	cherry tomatoes or plum tomatoes
1 cup	chopped shallots
1 tbsp	olive oil
1 cup	granulated sugar
1	sprig fresh thyme
1 tbsp	raspberry vinegar
1 tsp	cracked black peppercorns
¼ cup	vodka
¾ tsp	celery salt
1	small jalapeño pepper, seeded and finely chopped
¼ cup	each of finely diced celery, sweet red pepper and yellow pepper
¼ cup	freshly grated horseradish

SERVING SUGGESTION
This relish goes well when lightly heated with the wild boar pâté (page 18) or cold with any deli meats or cured game. It also makes a fine accompaniment to roasted quails, with celery, mushrooms and chestnuts.

1. Preheat oven to 350°F.

2. Wash the tomatoes and drain well. If using plum tomatoes, cut into halves.

3. Sauté the shallots in olive oil in a large shallow casserole until translucent, then add tomatoes, sugar and thyme. Sprinkle with vinegar and peppercorns.

4. Bake in the oven, uncovered, until the tomatoes are reduced and thick, about 2 to 3 hours.

5. Remove from oven and with a wooden spatula press the tomatoes through a fine mesh sieve. Return to the pot. Season with vodka, more vinegar (if the mixture seems to need a little more "pep") and celery salt.

6. Add the jalapeño to the tomatoes along with the celery, the peppers and horseradish. Reduce to a marmalade-like consistency.

7. Place in sterilized jars and store in the refrigerator.

Sun-Dried Cherry Relish

This wonderful recipe was devised by Ken Canavan, chef of our Cilantro restaurant.

MAKES 1½ CUPS

1 cup	sun-dried cherries (see page 86)
½ cup	sun-dried cranberries (see page 86)
1 cup	hot water
3 tbsp	finely diced red onion
1 tsp	tomato paste
1 tsp	ancho chili paste (see below)
4	cloves garlic, roasted
¼ cup	firmly packed brown sugar
1 tbsp	balsamic vinegar

SERVING SUGGESTION
Serve this with game such as venison steaks or antelope chops or with pork chops or baked ham.

1. Soak the cherries and cranberries in hot water for 5 minutes. Drain and rinse.

2. In a food processor combine berries, onion, tomato paste, ancho chili paste, garlic, sugar and vinegar. Process briefly, leaving berries fairly chunky.

3. Refrigerate relish. Will keep for 5 to 7 days.

ANCHO CHILI PASTE (MAKES ¾ CUP)

3	ancho chilies
⅓ cup	chicken stock (see page 70)
¼ cup	sour cream

1. Preheat oven to 350°F.
2. Slice along the length of each chili. Remove all visible seeds. Roast chilies in oven for 8 to 10 minutes, or until crisp.
3. Soak chilies in hot water, just to cover, for 15 minutes. Drain and pat dry.
4. Put chilies into a food processor with 2 tbsp of chicken stock. Purée chilies and add more chicken stock if needed. The texture should be that of paste.
5. Remove from processor and whisk in enough sour cream to make paste thick and creamy.
6. If using paste as a garnish, put mixture in a small squeeze bottle and create fancy designs.

Mustard Melons

Make this condiment at least one week before you plan to serve it.

MAKES 4 CUPS

3 tsp	dry mustard powder (e.g. Keens)
2 cups	water
2 cups	white vinegar
2¼ cups	granulated sugar
3½ lb	cantaloupe melon

SERVING SUGGESTION
Served cold, this goes well with cured meats; hot and lightly caramelized, it complements venison chops or roast pork.

1. In a ceramic or plastic container combine mustard powder, water, vinegar and sugar and mix well until sugar is dissolved.

2. Peel each cantaloupe and cut in half. Remove seeds and cut each half into 8 to 10 wedges. Place melon in the sugar/mustard mixture, cover and refrigerate for 7 days.

3. Transfer melons and liquid to a shallow pot and cook over high heat until melon is translucent and liquid thickens to the medium syrup stage (about 225°F on a candy thermometer). Spoon into sterilized jars and store in refrigerator.

Grainy Hot Black Mustard

The mustard seeds have to be soaked in water overnight and mustard should sit for 24 to 48 hours before being bottled.

MAKES 2 CUPS

½ cup	yellow mustard seeds
½ cup	black mustard seeds
½ cup	firmly packed brown sugar
2 tbsp	dry mustard powder (e.g. Keens)
¼ cup	black peppercorns, freshly crushed
⅓ cup	finely chopped chives
⅓ cup	finely chopped fresh basil
⅓ cup	finely chopped fresh oregano or thyme
3 inches	fresh horseradish
½ cup	apple cider
½ cup	white wine vinegar
1 tsp	turmeric (optional)
	Salt to taste

1. Soak mustard seeds in water overnight. Drain and grind in a food processor until a coarse paste forms.

2. Remove to a bowl and mix in brown sugar, mustard powder, peppercorns, chives, basil and oregano. Peel horseradish, grate finely and add to mixture. Mix well with wooden spatula.

3. Add apple cider and vinegar to give mixture a smooth but not runny consistency. Add turmeric for colour, if desired.

4. Season with salt to taste. Cover bowl and refrigerate for 24 to 48 hours.

5. Fill sterilized jars and seal with lid.

Garden Herb Salsa

Some of my friends add finely diced zucchini to give the salsa more texture.

MAKES ⅔ CUP

1	small jalapeño pepper
2	cloves garlic, finely chopped
1 tbsp	finely chopped Italian flat-leaf parsley
2 tbsp	finely chopped coriander
2 tbsp	finely chopped chervil
1 tbsp	finely chopped mint
2 tbsp	finely chopped chives
3 tbsp	cold-pressed sunflower seed oil
½ tsp	grated lime zest
1	lime
1	small shallot, finely diced (optional)

1. Remove seeds from jalapeño pepper and chop finely. Combine with garlic, parsley, coriander, chervil, mint, chives, oil, lime zest and juice of l lime (or according to taste). Mix well.

2. Add diced shallots, if you wish.

Honey Spiced Nuts

MAKES 4 CUPS

4 cups	mixed nuts (approx. 1½ lb), such as pecans, almonds, cashews
½ cup	liquid honey
1 tsp	freshly ground black pepper
1 tsp	chili powder
1 tsp	ground cumin
1 tsp	ground coriander
¼ tsp	ground nutmeg
¼ tsp	ground cinnamon
1	pinch blackening spices (see page 85)

1. Preheat oven to 350°F.
2. Toast nuts for 5 to 7 minutes.
3. In a large bowl combine honey, pepper, chili powder, cumin, coriander, nutmeg, cinnamon and blackening spices. Add nuts and toss.
4. Place nuts on a parchment- or foil-lined cookie sheet and toast again for 5 to 10 minutes. Stir occasionally. Be careful not to overcook.
5. Remove from oven, allow to cool and separate nuts. Store in a tin or glass jar in a dry spot, not in the refrigerator.

Gingerbread Spices

Here are two gingerbread spice recipes from my mother. She always mixed her own, rather than using commercial mixes.

I suggest you buy whole spices and grind them in a spice mill or a clean coffee grinder. Adjust the spice mill to the finest setting, grind whole spices and transfer to a jar or tin with a tight-fitting lid. Use these mixes carefully as the flavours are very intense.

MIX A (FOR BAKED GOODS SUCH AS ALMOND COOKIES)

1 tsp	cardamom seeds
½ tsp	fennel seeds
½ tsp	white peppercorns
10 tsp	ground cinnamon
2 tsp	ground nutmeg
1 tsp	ground cloves
2 tsp	ground ginger

1. Grind separately cardamom and fennel seeds and peppercorns. Combine with cinnamon, nutmeg, cloves and ginger and mix well. Sift through a fine sieve and, if necessary, grind the coarser bits again and add to mixture.

2. Store in an airtight container.

MIX B (FOR GINGERBREAD, GAME, GOOSE, DUCK AND PORK)

10 tsp	whole anise seeds
5 tsp	coriander seeds
1 tsp	fennel seeds
½ tsp	vanilla bean seeds
½ tsp	white peppercorns
10 tsp	ground cinnamon
2 tsp	ground ginger
¾ tsp	ground nutmeg

1. Grind separately anise, coriander, fennel and vanilla bean seeds and peppercorns. Combine with cinnamon, ginger and nutmeg and mix well. Sift through a fine sieve and, if necessary, grind the coarser bits again and add to mixture.

2. Store in an airtight container.

Blackening Spice Mix

MAKES ⅓ CUP

2 tbsp	paprika
1 tbsp	salt
2 tsp	onion powder
2 tsp	garlic powder
1 tbsp	cayenne pepper
2 tsp	freshly ground white pepper
1 tsp	freshly ground black pepper
2 tsp	dried thyme
2 tsp	dried oregano

1. In a small bowl combine all the ingredients and mix well.
2. Store in an airtight container.

Crème Fraîche

MAKES 3 CUPS

2 cups	whipping cream
1 cup	sour cream

1. In a non-metallic bowl stir together whipping cream and sour cream. Cover with plastic wrap.
2. Allow to rest at room temperature for 16 to 24 hours, or until thickened.
3. Refrigerate for 24 hours before using.

Dried Fruits and Vegetables

You can dry almost any fruit or vegetable, but some work better than others. Important factors are good quality produce, time and a little patience. Your first batch may not work out as well as expected, but you'll soon master the technique.

One advantage of drying your own produce is cost. Dried cherries, for example, are available in specialty stores but are rather expensive. They also may contain sulphites, which are added to improve the colour.

Fruits and vegetables can be dried in the sun or in an oven or dryer.

The dryer can be a commercial one or one which you have made yourself — a simple box vented on the top and bottom and fitted with several screen about 12 inches by 12 inches, as well as a lightbulb with a dimmer-control switch.

With a commercial dryer, follow the manufacturer's directions.

With a home-built dryer, place the fruits or vegetables on the screens. For the first day set the 100-watt bulb on full; then lower it to 50 watts.

With an oven, use warm or lowest setting.

With sun, place produce on parchment paper and keep in full sunlight during the day.

PRODUCE	PREPARATION	APPROXIMATE DRYING TIME
Cherries	Cut into halves and place skin side down on parchment or screen	4 to 5 hours, up to full day
Cranberries, blueberries, huckleberries	Use only ripe fruit. Wash if necessary and leave whole.(Do not use frozen fruit, as juices are lost during defrosting.)	4 to 5 hours, up to full day
Rosehips	Pick only after a frost. Remove any dry petals and cut into halves. Dry either with or without seeds.	1 day

Fruits with stones	Cut small fruit into halves, larger ones into quarters or wedges. Place skin side down first and turn frequently.	2 to 3 days
Mushrooms	Leave very small ones whole, cut others into halves or quarters. Cut very large ones into slices, not too thin.	4 to 6 hours each day for 2 days
Green beans	Wash beans and dry them whole. They are extremely tasty in winter dishes, rehydrated and served with hearty roasts, smoked pork or sausages.	4 to 6 days in sun (works best)
Tomatoes	Plum tomatoes work well and are very tasty. Cut into halves and squeeze out seeds and some juice. Place skin side down for the first day.	2 to 3 days
Chilies	I have only used the following technique to dry chilies: Hang whole branches upside down in a shady spot for about one week. Pick off dry peppers and if necessary finish off drying in the sun for a day or so.	
Apples, pears	Slice very thinly, sprinkle one side with icing sugar and place on a very lightly oiled tray. Place in oven to dry, but do not allow them to take on any colour. Remove slices to a rack to cool. They should be very crisp and brittle.	3 to 4 hours in warm oven

COOKIES AND BARS

Lemon Cornmeal and Currant Biscotti

MAKES 28 TO 30

1 cup	currants
1 cup	dried apricots, coarsely chopped
1	lemon
½ cup	unsalted butter
¾ cup	granulated sugar
½ cup	stone-ground yellow cornmeal
1 tsp	pure vanilla extract
2	large eggs, lightly beaten
1½ tsp	baking powder
¼ tsp	salt
¼ tsp	ground nutmeg
2¼ cups	all-purpose flour

1. Preheat oven to 350°F.
2. Place currants and apricots in a bowl and cover with very hot water for 5 minutes. Drain, dry well and set aside.
3. Grate the zest from the lemon and squeeze out the juice.
4. In a large bowl cream the butter with sugar and cornmeal. Stir in the vanilla, lemon zest and lemon juice. Blend in eggs.
5. In a separate bowl mix together the baking powder, salt, nutmeg and flour and fold dry ingredients into butter mixture. Fold in apricots and currants.
6. With floured hands spread and shape batter into two 8- by 10-inch logs. Flatten slightly and bake on a parchment-lined baking sheet until lightly browed and set, about 25 to 30 minutes. Remove and let cool.
7. With a serrated knife cut loaves into ¾-inch slices. Reduce heat to 325°F and bake for a further 15 to 20 minutes until cookies are dry. Turn biscuits once during baking to brown evenly. Remove and cool on wire rack.

Mountain Guide Biscotti

MAKES 14

6 tbsp	unsalted butter, melted
6 tbsp	vegetable oil
½ cup	granulated sugar
¼ cup	firmly packed brown sugar
1½ tsp	pure vanilla extract
3	large eggs, lightly beaten
3 cups	all-purpose flour
1¾ tsp	baking powder
¼ tsp	salt
1½ cups	coarsely chopped honey and almond nougat milk chocolate bar (e.g. Toblerone)
¼ cup	whole pecans

1. Preheat oven to 350°F.

2. In a mixing bowl cream the butter, oil and sugars until well blended. Stir in vanilla. Blend in eggs.

3. In a separate bowl mix together flour, baking powder and salt. Fold dry ingredients into butter mixture and blend well. Fold in chocolate and pecans.

4. Place batter on a large parchment-lined baking sheet (batter will be thick and sticky) and form into two 8- by 3-inch logs. Flour hands as needed in order to shape dough. Bake in oven until set, about 25 minutes. Remove and let cool for 15 minutes.

5. Transfer to a cutting board and cut into ¾-inch diagonal slices. Place slices on baking sheet and bake on one side for 12 minutes. Turn over and bake other side for about 5 minutes, or until cookies are dry. Remove and cool on wire rack.

Going Nuts Biscotti

Makes 24 to 30

7 oz	almond paste or marzipan
1¾ cups	granulated sugar
½ cup	unsalted butter
¼ cup	finely chopped almonds
¼ cup	ground hazelnuts
¼ cup	chopped pecans
¼ cup	whole pine nuts
4	eggs, lightly beaten
1 tsp	pure vanilla extract
2 tsp	almond extract
¼ tsp	salt
⅛ tsp	ground cinnamon
½ tsp	baking soda
1 tsp	baking powder
3 cups	all-purpose flour
1 cup	whole blanched almonds

1. Preheat oven to 350°F.

2. With a vegetable grater shred almond paste. In a mixing bowl cream the almond paste and sugar together, then add the butter. Cream until smooth. Stir in the almonds, hazelnuts, pecans and pine nuts. Blend in eggs, vanilla and almond extract.

3. In a separate bowl mix together the salt, cinnamon, baking soda, baking powder and flour. Fold this into the egg mixture and blend well. Fold in whole almonds.

4. Spoon out one-third of the batter onto a parchment-lined baking sheet. The batter will seem quite loose abut should be roughly 8 inches by 4 inches. Repeat twice more.

5. Bake about 40 minutes, until dough is golden and seems dry to the touch. If dough browns too quickly, reduce oven heat to 325°F and bake a little longer. Remove from oven and cool for 15 minutes. Transfer to a cutting board and with a serrated knife cut into slices, slightly on the diagonal, about ½- to ¾-inch thick.

6. Whole almonds can make the cutting difficult. An alternative method is to freeze the dough for one hour after the first baking, then cut.

7. Reduce oven temperature to 300°F and return slices to baking sheets. Bake for another 35 to 45 minutes or longer until brown and crisp. Turn once during baking. Remove and cool on wire rack.

Fireweed Honey Cookies

MAKES 4 DOZEN

2 cups	all-purpose flour
¼ cup	wheat germ
1½ tsp	baking powder
¼ tsp	salt
⅓ cup	fireweed honey or other aromatic honey, such as clover, lavender, lindenflower
¾ cup	unsalted butter
2	egg yolks
¼ cup	milk
1 tsp	pure vanilla extract
1 cup	chopped pumpkin seeds

1. Preheat oven to 375°F.

2. In a bowl mix together flour, wheat germ, baking powder and salt. Add honey and butter. When the mixture is crumbly, add egg yolks, milk and vanilla.

3. Knead dough until smooth. For each cookie, shape a rounded tablespoon of dough into an oval loaf. Roll in chopped pumpkin seeds.

4. Bake on a parchment-lined cookie sheet in the oven for 15 to 20 minutes. Remove and cool on wire rack.

Buffalo Chip Cookies

MAKES 3 ½ DOZEN

1 cup	unsalted butter
½ cup	firmly packed brown sugar
¼ cup	granulated sugar
1	egg, lightly beaten
½ tsp	pure vanilla extract
1¼ cups	rolled oats
1 cup	all-purpose flour
½ tsp	baking soda
1½ tsp	baking powder
½ tsp	salt
½ cup	chopped honey and almond nougat milk chocolate bar (e.g. Toblerone)
½ cup	chopped pecans

1. In a bowl cream the butter and add sugars. Add egg and vanilla.
2. Process the rolled oats in a food processor to a fine flour.
3. Mix together the rolled oats, flour, baking soda, baking powder and salt and add to the creamed butter. Fold in the chocolate bar pieces and pecans.
4. Chill about 45 minutes. Roll into logs and wrap in plastic wrap. Chill at least 2 hours or overnight.
5. Preheat oven to 350°F.
6. Slice the logs into ¼-inch slices. Place on a parchment-lined cookie sheet and bake in oven for 6 to 7 minutes. Remove and cool on wire rack.

Cranberry Sesame Cookies

MAKES 4 DOZEN

1¼ cups	all-purpose flour
½ tsp	baking soda
½ tsp	salt
1 tsp	ground cinnamon
¾ cup	chopped frozen or fresh cranberries
½ cup	vegetable oil
1 cup	granulated sugar
1	egg, lightly beaten
1¼ cups	rolled oats
1 cup	sesame seeds
¼ cup	milk

1. Preheat oven to 375°F.
2. Sift flour with baking soda, salt and cinnamon. Stir in cranberries.
3. In a separate bowl, beat together the oil, sugar and egg. Add rolled oats, sesame seeds and milk.
4. Gradually beat flour mixture into egg mixture and stir until dough is thoroughly blended.
5. Drop dough by heaping teaspoonfuls onto a parchment-lined cookie sheet allowing room for cookies to spread. Bake in oven for 10 to 12 minutes. Remove and cool on wire rack.

Winter "Things" Cookies

MAKES 5 DOZEN

½ cup	water
1½–2 cups	dried fruit (equal parts of any combination of dried cranberries, cherries, figs, apricots, prunes, raisins and candied ginger, see page 86)
½ cup	vegetable shortening
1 cup	firmly packed brown sugar
2	large eggs
½ tsp	pure vanilla extract
½ cup	chopped walnuts
2 cups	all-purpose flour
½ tsp	baking powder
½ tsp	baking soda
1 tsp	salt
½ tsp	ground cinnamon
¼ tsp	ground nutmeg
¼ tsp	ground allspice

1. Preheat oven to 350°F.
2. In a saucepan combine water and dried fruit and boil for 5 minutes. Remove from heat and let cool.
3. In a bowl cream shortening with sugar, add eggs, vanilla, cooled fruit and nuts.
4. In a separate bowl combine flour, baking powder, baking soda, salt, cinnamon, nutmeg and allspice. Add to creamed shortening and blend well.
5. Drop by teaspoonfuls onto parchment-lined baking sheets and bake in oven for 8 to 10 minutes. Remove and cool on wire rack.

Rocky Mountain Hermits

MAKES 4 ½ DOZEN

¾ cup	vegetable shortening
1 cup	firmly packed brown sugar
1	large egg, lightly beaten
½ cup	dried cranberries (see page 86)
2 cups	all-purpose flour
½ tsp	baking soda
½ tsp	salt
½ tsp	ground cinnamon
½ tsp	ground nutmeg
¼ cup	cold strong coffee
½ cup	chopped hazelnuts

1. Preheat oven to 400°F.

2. In a mixing bowl cream together the shortening and sugar and add egg.

3. In a separate bowl combine flour, baking soda, salt, cinnamon and nutmeg and blend well. Fold the dry ingredients into the creamed shortening alternately with coffee. Blend well. Fold in cranberries and nuts.

4. Drop by teaspoonfuls onto a greased baking sheet and bake in oven for 10 minutes. Remove and cool on wire rack.

Grizzly Granola Bars

MAKES 3 DOZEN

1 cup	unsalted butter
1 cup	firmly packed brown sugar
2	large eggs
¼ cup	molasses
1 tsp	pure vanilla extract
1¾ cups	all-purpose flour
½ tsp	baking soda
½ tsp	salt
1½ cups	rolled oats
¾ cup	wheat germ
¾ cup	dessicated or angelflake coconut
¾ cup	sunflower seeds
¾ cup	chopped dried fruit (any one or combination of cranberries, cherries, figs, raisins, apricots, see page 86)
⅓ cup	pistachio nuts or pumpkin seeds

1. Preheat oven to 350°F.
2. In a bowl cream together the butter with the sugar. Add eggs, molasses and vanilla.
3. In a separate bowl sift together the flour, baking soda, salt and powdered milk. Add to the butter mixture and blend well. Add rolled oats, wheat germ, coconut, sunflower seeds, dried fruit and pistachio nuts and mix well.
4. Spread in a greased 9- by 13-inch pan and bake for 20 to 25 minutes or until golden. Remove from oven, cool and cut into bars.

Summer Hiking Bars

MAKES 16

½ cup	salted butter, softened
½ cup	unsalted butter, softened
⅓ cup	firmly packed brown sugar
2	egg yolks
2 cups	all-purpose flour
1 cup	raspberry jam
4 tbsp	confectioner's sugar
½ cup	chopped pecans

1. Preheat oven to 375°F.

2. In a mixing bowl cream the butters and sugar. Beat in egg yolks. Sift in flour, half a cup at a time.

3. Press half the dough into an ungreased 9- by 9-inch baking pan. Spread with jam and top with remaining dough, patting evenly. Sprinkle with confectioner's sugar and nuts. Bake in oven for 35 minutes.

4. Remove, cool and cut into bars.

DESSERTS

Cranberry Rhubarb Pot Pie with Bitter-Orange Ice Cream

2 cups	granulated sugar
3 cups	fresh or frozen cranberries
3 cups	fresh or frozen chopped rhubarb
1 cup	fresh orange juice
1	orange
1	vanilla bean
1	stick cinnamon
½ tsp	cracked black peppercorns
2 tsp	finely chopped fresh ginger
2 cups	all-purpose flour
1 tsp	baking powder
½ tsp	salt
¼ cup	granulated sugar
½ cup	unsalted butter, cold
¾ cup	buttermilk
1	large egg
1 tbsp	water
1 tbsp	granulated sugar

1. Sprinkle 2 cups of the sugar over the bottom of a large saucepan. Cook on medium-high heat without stirring until sugar liquefies and turns a deep caramel colour. Add cranberries, rhubarb and orange juice and bring to a boil.

2. Grate the zest of one orange and add to pot along with vanilla, cinnamon, pepper and ginger. Do not worry if caramel is lumpy; it will melt as the mixture cooks.

3. Reduce heat and cook until cranberries pop and mixture is thick and jam-like, about 15 minutes. Remove vanilla bean and cinnamon stick and cool.

4. Preheat oven to 350°F.

5. In a bowl combine flour, baking powder, salt and ¼ cup of the sugar. Cut in butter to resemble coarse meal. Add buttermilk and mix just enough to form a ball. Immediately turn out onto a floured surface and roll out dough to ¼-inch thickness. Cut into desired shapes.

6. Place filling in a medium-deep pie plate and cover top with cut-outs of dough. Brush top with mixture of egg and water and sprinkle with 1 tbsp of sugar.

7. Bake in oven for 25 to 30 minutes or until golden. Serve with bitter-orange ice cream. (recipe below)

BITTER-ORANGE ICE CREAM (MAKES 3½ CUPS)

1	orange
1 cup	fresh orange juice
1 cup	whipping cream
1½ cups	milk
1	vanilla bean
4	egg yolks
½ cup	granulated sugar

1. Grate the zest of one orange and place in a small saucepan with the orange juice. Heat over medium-high heat until mixture is reduced to ½ cup. Set aside.

2. In a saucepan place cream and milk. Split open the vanilla bean and scrape pulp into milk. Heat gently until mixture comes to the boil. Simmer for 5 minutes, then remove from heat. Gradually stir in orange juice mixture.

3. In a heatproof bowl beat egg yolks with sugar until pale and thick. Beat in hot vanilla mixture. Place bowl over pot of simmering water — water should not be touching bottom of bowl. Cook gently, stirring constantly until mixture thickens slightly. DO NOT BOIL. Strain and cool mixture completely.

4. Place mixture in an ice-cream maker and freeze according to manufacturer's instructions.

Bailey's White Chocolate Strawberry Cheesecake

SERVES 10 TO 12

1	lemon
1½ cups	graham cracker crumbs
½ cup	granulated sugar
7 tbsp	melted unsalted butter
5 oz	white chocolate
1½ lb	cream cheese
⅔ cup	icing sugar
4	large eggs
⅓ cup	Bailey's Irish Cream
1 cup	sour cream
1 pint	fresh strawberries
2 cups	whipping cream
1 tsp	granulated sugar
	Fresh mint for garnish

SERVING SUGGESTION
Drizzle some extra Bailey's Irish Cream on top of the completed dish.

1. Grate the zest of the lemon and mix together with graham cracker crumbs, sugar and 3 tbsp of the melted butter. Press mixture onto the bottom of a greased 9-inch springform pan.

2. Preheat oven to 350°F.

3. In a double boiler very carefully melt chocolate over low heat. Remove and cool to room temperature.

4. In a bowl beat together the cream cheese and icing sugar until smooth. Beat in the eggs, one at a time. Stir in the cooled chocolate. Add Bailey's Irish Cream, the remaining 4 tbsp of melted butter and sour cream. Blend well.

5. Pour over the crust in the springform pan and bake in the centre of the oven for 45 minutes.

6. Turn off heat and prop open the oven door until cheesecake reaches room temperature. Remove and refrigerate overnight.

7. To serve, remove the cake from the pan and cut into 10 or 12 pieces. Wash and slice strawberries. Lightly sweeten whipping cream with 1 tsp of sugar and whip to soft peaks. Arrange cake on plates and generously heap strawberries on top. Spoon whipped cream on side of strawberries. Garnish with sprigs of mint.

Almond Tuilles

This recipe was given to me by my mentor, Martin Fopp, former chef of the Beau Rivage Palace Hotel in Lausanne, Switzerland. I like to serve the tuilles with sorbet or light fruit gratins.

The batter needs to rest for at least 8 hours, so prepare it one day in advance.

MAKES 12

4	large eggs
1½ cups	icing sugar
2	vanilla beans
1 tsp	cornstarch
¼ cup	unsalted butter
8 oz	sliced blanched almonds

1. Beat eggs lightly and add sugar, the pulp of the vanilla beans, cornstarch and butter. Pour over almonds, mix well and refrigerate for at least 8 hours or overnight.

2. Preheat oven to 350°F.

3. Mix the batter once more; the almonds may have settled. On a parchment-lined baking sheet spread a soupspoon full of batter and thin out to a circle about 4 inches in diameter. Bake only 4 or 5 at one time.

4. When tuilles are golden, remove with a wide spatula and drape over a rolling pin until they hold their shape. Serve when completely cool and hardened. These tuilles are fragile and will keep for only about one day. They should be placed on a large plate. Do not wrap or refrigerate them.

Apple Tart with Cider Sorbet

SERVES 8

⅓ cup	salted butter, cold
1⅛ cup	all-purpose flour
⅔ cup	icing sugar
1	large egg
1 tbsp	water
3	tart apples, such as Granny Smith or Boskoop
1 tbsp	lemon juice
1 tbsp	granulated sugar
3 tbsp	melted unsalted butter
3 – 4 tbsp	apple jelly
⅓ cup	apple brandy (e.g. Calvados or Apfelkorn)

1. Dice the butter into ¼-inch cubes and combine with the flour, icing sugar and egg to form a dough. Work ingredients together with your fingers, but do not overwork. If necessary, sprinkle some water into the dough. Form into a roll and refrigerate for 1 to 2 hours.

2. Preheat oven to 350°F.

3. Roll out dough to a thickness of about ⅛ inch and line an 11-inch flan plan with a removable bottom. Bake in oven for 10 to 15 minutes. Remove from oven as soon as pastry becomes a little coloured. Prick any bubbles in pastry with fork.

6. Increase oven temperature to 375°F.

7. Peel apples and cut into quarters. Remove seeds and slice each quarter into 5 to 6 wedges. Toss with lemon juice and arrange in an overlapping circular pattern on the pre-baked crust. Sprinkle sugar evenly over top. Drizzle buttter over the apples and bake in oven, on upper rack, for another 30 minutes. Remove and cool a little.

8. Melt apple jelly with apple brandy. Brush apples with jelly mixture and let tart cool to room temperature.

9. Serve with cider sorbet (recipe next page).

CIDER SORBET

1 cup	granulated sugar
1 cup	water
1 cup	Granny Smith or MacIntosh apple cider
2 tbsp	apple brandy (e.g. Calvados or Apfelkorn)

1. Make sugar syrup by boiling together sugar and water for 3 to 5 minutes. Scoop off any foam.
2. Stir together syrup, apple cider and apple brandy. Place in an ice-cream maker and freeze according to manufacturer's instructions.

Bittersweet Chocolate Cake with Pears and Coffee Sauce

This cake and the coffee sauce that is served with it must be made at least one day in advance.

SERVES 6 TO 8

2 tbsp	icing sugar
1 cup	crushed oatmeal cookies
⅓ cup	toasted ground hazelnuts
¼ cup	unsalted butter, melted
¼ tsp	ground cinnamon
1¾ cups	granulated sugar
¾ cup	cocoa powder
5	gelatin leaves or 1 envelope of gelatin
2 tbsp	dark rum or pear brandy (Williamine), warmed
1	orange (optional)
¾ cup	milk
1	pinch salt
¼	vanilla bean
3	fresh pears or 1 tin Bartlett pears, well drained
2 cups	water
1	lemon
2 cups	whipping cream
	Sprig of fresh mint for garnish
	Cocoa powder for dusting

SERVING SUGGESTION
You can substitute fresh berries or Summer Berry Sauce (see page 115) for the coffee sauce.

1. With your fingers lightly oil a cake ring without a bottom. Dust with icing sugar. This will give the cake very smooth sides and will allow the ring to slide off easily.

2. Set the ring on your serving platter.

3. In a bowl mix together the crushed cookies, hazelnuts, melted butter and cinnamon. Press mixture firmly in cake ring and chill for at least 20 minutes.

4. Sift together ¾ cup of the sugar and all of the cocoa powder. Set aside.

5. Soak the gelatin leaves in cold water until soft, about 5 to 10 minutes. Squeeze out water and melt gelatin in the warmed rum. If you are using an envelope of gelatin, place ¼ cup of water in a small saucepan and sprinkle in gelatin. Allow it to rest for 5 minutes and heat gently to dissolve gelatin. If you are using orange, grate the zest and squeeze the juice of one orange. Add to gelatin.

6. In a wide pot combine milk with salt and add vanilla bean which has been cut open and scraped. Bring to a boil. As soon as the milk begins to boil, remove the vanilla bean and add the cocoa mixture all at once. Stir constantly with a whisk until cocoa is dissolved and the mixture comes to a boil and thickens.

7. Remove from heat and cool for a few minutes. Stir in gelatin mixture and let cool to room temperature.

8. For fresh pears, bring to a boil 2 cups of water, 1 cup of sugar and the juice of one lemon. Peel the pears, cut into halves and remove each stem and core. Add to syrup and simmer for 6 to 10 minutes. The pears are ready when they are cooked through but still firm. Test with a toothpick. Remove from heat and chill. Pat the pears dry on kitchen towels. The pears can be prepared in advance.

9. Whip the cream. If you are worried about using cream, you can reduce the amount to one cup and substitute the other cup with 4 beaten egg whites. (You will use the yolks in the coffee sauce.) Stir the cocoa mixture once it has reached room temperature and fold in whipped cream.

10. Arrange the pear halves in a circle, with smaller ends in the centre, on the cookie crust. Spread the whipped cream mixture over the pears and with a wet spatula or knife smooth the top. Chill in refrigerator for at least 12 hours or overnight.

11. Remove cake ring and decorate with mint and/or dust with cocoa powder. Serve with coffee sauce (recipe below).

COFFEE SAUCE

⅔ cup	milk
3 tbsp	whole espresso coffee beans
4	egg yolks
¼ cup	granulated sugar

1. In a saucepan bring milk to a boil and pour over the coffee beans. Cover and keep at room temperature overnight.
2. Strain off milk and heat in a double boiler.
3. Combine egg yolks and sugar and add to hot milk. Cook gently until mixture thickens. Strain again and cool.

Hazelnut Parfait with Fresh Cherries

This recipe produces about 2½ cups of sauce, more than is required for this dish, but the extra will keep in the refrigerator for several days.

SERVES 4

FOR HAZELNUT PARFAIT

⅔ cup	granulated sugar
2 tbsp	finely chopped hazelnuts
4	egg yolks
¼ cup	honey
½ cup	hot milk
⅓ cup	whipped cream

FOR CHERRIES

½	lemon
½	orange
¼ cup	Merlot wine
¾ cup	granulated sugar
1	small stick cinnamon
1 lb	dark ripe cherries

1. In a small pan melt ⅓ cup of sugar until golden caramel in colour. Stir in the nuts and transfer immediately to an oiled baking sheet. Cool and chop finely.

2. Whip the egg yolks with ⅓ cup of sugar and honey until light and fluffy. Place in the top of a double boiler and add hot milk, stirring constantly. Cook until thickened. Do not allow mixture to boil or eggs will curdle. Remove from heat and cool.

3. Add chopped caramelized nuts and whipped cream to the cooled mixture. Fill 4 4-oz ramekins and freeze for 4 to 5 hours until firm.

4. Grate the zest of ½ lemon and ½ orange.

5. Boil Merlot with ¾ cup of sugar, lemon zest, orange zest and cinnamon stick for 10 minutes.

6. Wash cherries and remove stems.

7. Remove wine from heat and add cherries. Return to heat and cook for 10 minutes more. Remove cherries and cinnamon stick. Reduce sauce to ½ cup, return cherries to sauce. The juice from the cherries will increase the volume.

8. Remove ramekins from freezer and dip quickly into hot water. Loosen the parfait with a paring knife and turn out onto plates. Arrange warm cherries around parfait.

Christmas Pudding

The pudding mix should be made at least one month before cooking.

MAKES 8 INDIVIDUAL PUDDINGS OR 1 LARGE

2	oranges
2	lemons
¾ cup	raisins
½ cup	pitted prunes, finely diced
2	apples (Gala, Cox's Orange Pippin or MacIntosh) peeled, cored and diced
⅔ cup	sliced almonds
2 tbsp	candied orange peel
¼ tsp	ground cinnamon
¼ tsp	ground ginger
2 tbsp	candied lemon peel
⅛ tsp	ground nutmeg
1 cup	granulated sugar
2	large eggs
¼ cup	sweet sherry
1 tbsp	rum
1 tbsp	Port
1 tbsp	brandy
1 tbsp	Marsala wine
2 tbsp	Madeira wine
¼ cup	dark beer
5 cups	finely diced white bread, crusts removed
¼ cup	vegetable shortening
⅓ cup	all-purpose flour

SERVING SUGGESTION
I like Brandied Berries with this pudding (see page 113).

1. Grate the zest of the oranges and lemons and squeeze out the juices. In a large bowl mix the zest and juice with all the other ingredients. Blend well.

2. Transfer mixture to a non-metallic container with a lid. Cover container with plastic wrap, place lid on top and refrigerate for at least one month.

3. On the day that you decide to steam the pudding, preheat oven to 350°F.

4. Remove pudding from refrigerator and stir mixture with a wooden spoon. Fill individual pudding basins which have been lightly oiled or buttered. Cover basins with lids or foil and place in a large casserole dish.

5. Fill the casserole with water so that the level reaches halfway up the sides of the basins. Poach the puddings in the oven for about 45 minutes.

6. Remove from basins and serve with your favourite topping.

Pear Strudel with Plum Sauce and Caramel Ice Cream

SERVES 6

6	pears, preferably William or Bosc
2 tbsp	lemon juice
8 tbsp	granulated sugar
4 tbsp	raisins
4 tbsp	sliced almonds
1	pinch ground cinnamon
4 tbsp	pear brandy (Williamine)
2 tbsp	graham cracker crumbs (optional)
1	package phyllo pastry, defrosted
½ cup	unsalted butter, melted
2 tbsp	icing sugar
1 cup	diced ripe prune plums
¾ cup	dry red wine
1	stick cinnamon

1. Peel pears, core and cut into thin slices. Drizzle lemon juice over pears and toss fruit in 4 tbsp of the sugar, raisins, ground cinnamon, almonds, pear brandy and graham cracker crumbs. Mix well and set aside.

2. Remove one sheet of phyllo pastry and place on dry work surface. Overlap a second sheet on the first to form a sheet about 4 inches longer than your baking tray.

3. Brush the pastry with melted butter. Repeat procedure with four more layers. Brush the top layer with melted butter.

4. Place pear filling on the pastry, leaving at least 2 inches of pastry border on all sides. Place the rectangle of pastry so that the long sides are to your left and right. Fold in the flaps on the two long sides and tightly roll up strudel, starting at the end closest to you.

5. Preheat oven to 375°F.

6. Place strudel, seam side down, onto a parchment-lined baking sheet and brush remaining melted butter on pastry.

7. Bake in oven for 25 to 30 minutes or until golden brown and crisp on top.

8. While strudel is baking, make sauce. In a saucepan combine plums, the remaining 4 tbsp of sugar, red wine and cinnamon stick. Simmer until plums are soft. Remove cinnamon stick and let sauce cool. Purée the sauce in a blender, strain and set aside.

9. Remove strudel from oven, let cool a little and dust with icing sugar. Cut into portions and serve warm. Place two slices of strudel on each plate, spoon a little sauce on one side with a scoop of caramel ice cream (recipe below).

CARAMEL ICE CREAM

½	vanilla bean
1 cup	whipping cream
½ cup	milk
1 cup	granulated sugar
5	egg yolks

1. Cut vanilla bean in half and scrape out pulp. Add pulp to the cream and milk and simmer the mixture for 5 minutes, then set aside.

2. In a large saucepan put in a small amount of sugar and melt it. Continue adding sugar until it reaches a golden caramel colour. Stir constantly with wooden spoon. Once all the sugar is melted, add the milk mixture and stir until all sugar is dissolved.

3. Beat the egg yolks until creamy and add to hot milk mixture. Place bowl over a pot of simmering water, making sure that the bottom of the bowl does not touch the water. Gently stir until the mixture becomes creamy and thickens slightly.

4. Strain into a bowl and cool off. Freeze in ice-cream maker according to manufacturer's instructions.

5. This produces a soft ice cream because of the amount of caramel.

Lemon Tart with Red Fruits

SERVES 4 TO 6

4	large eggs
1¼ cups	granulated sugar
1¾ cups	all-purpose flour
⅔ cup	ground hazelnuts
1	pinch salt
1 cup	unsalted butter, at room temperature
3	egg yolks
4	medium lemons
3 tbsp	crème fraîche (see page 85)
	Red berries for garnish

1. In a bowl whisk one egg and ½ cup of sugar until mixture thickens. Add the flour, hazelnuts and a pinch of salt and mix in until it resembles coarse meal. Work in ½ cup of the butter and mix to a firm dough. Let dough rest for 30 to 40 minutes.

2. Preheat oven to 375°F.

3. Roll out dough and line an 11-inch fluted flan pan. Prick the dough with a fork and weigh it down with a layer of foil and beans or weights. Bake blind for 20 minutes, removing the weights for the last 5 minutes of cooking time. Remove and let shell cool.

4. Reduce oven temperature to 325°F.

5. Cream the remaining ½ cup of butter with ¾ cup of sugar until fluffy and pale. Beat together 3 eggs and 3 yolks and gradually work them into the butter.

6. Grate the zest of the lemons and squeeze out juice. If you prefer a less tart flavour, reduce the number of lemons to three. Add zest and crème fraîche to butter and stir in the juice. Don't worry if the mixture looks as though it has curdled.

7. Pour filling into the baked shell, place shell on a jelly roll pan and bake for 45 to 50 minutes until centre is set. Remove from oven and cool.

8. If you wish, dust with icing sugar. Serve on plates garnished with red berries.

Brandied Berries

This is a variation on the rumtopf or pot of rum, a traditional dessert in Europe. Starting with summer berries, layers of fruit and sugar are added to a large earthenware crock and topped up with rum. By Christmas, one has a potent dessert to battle the cold.

   I prefer to use only summer berries and to shorten the marination time.

Equal parts of summer berries such as strawberries, raspberries, blackberries, blueberries, loganberries, saskatoon berries, gooseberries, red, white and black currants (no kiwis, please)

1 lb icing sugar for each pound of fruit.

½ bottle brandy, white or dark rum or equal parts of plum brandy (slivovitz), kirsch and framboise for each pound of fruit

SERVING SUGGESTION
These berries are delicious over ice cream, cheesecake or when used as a base for a kir or a martini.

1. Clean berries, but, if possible, do not wash them. Remove stems and leaves.

2. In a large ceramic container arrange the fruit in alternating layers with a sprinkling of icing sugar between layers. Cover the container and allow fruit to settle for one day.

3. Pour brandy or rum on the fruit, cover with a lid or a plate and place in a cool place for at least one week. Do not refrigerate.

4. Stir gently and serve.

Warm Potato Cakes with Raspberries

It's important to use baking potatoes which cook up flaky rather than red skin or firm cooking potatoes.

SERVES 6

2	Idaho potatoes (about 8 oz each)
3	large eggs, separated
⅓ cup	granulated sugar
½	lemon
½	vanilla bean pulp
½ lb	raspberries or (wild) strawberries
2 tbsp	raspberry liqueur
2 – 3 tbsp	icing sugar
⅓ cup	plain yogurt
6	sprigs fresh mint leaves
	Icing sugar for garnish

1. Steam potatoes in their skins (or boil and drain) and let them dry off a little. Peel them while they are still hot and finely grate or press through a fine ricer. Allow potatoes to dry, uncovered, for about 2 hours. Measure out 1 ½ cups and set aside.

2. In a bowl mix ¼ cup of the granulated sugar with 3 egg yolks, vanilla and the grated zest of the lemon. Stir until sugar is completely dissolved but do not whip.

3. With a hand-held blender or portable mixer blend sugar mixture into the potatoes.

4. Whip the 3 egg whites with the remaining granulated sugar to a meringue and fold into the potato mixture.

5. Lightly butter 6 ramekins (about 3 inches in diameter) and place in refrigerator until butter is firm. This will make it easier to remove the potato cakes later.

6. Preheat oven to 400°F.

7. Fill the ramekins with the potato mixture and set in a pan filled with 1 inch of hot water. Bake in oven, uncovered, for 30 to 35 minutes.

8. Purée half the berries with the liqueur and season to taste with icing sugar.

9. Drape sauce on each plate and decorate with yogurt which has been lightly stirred. Garnish with the rest of the berries and mint leaves.

10. Remove potato cakes from the ramekins by turning them out carefully onto your hand. Place them, right side up, on the decorated plates and dust lightly with icing sugar. Serve at once.

Summer Berry Sauce

This simple recipe will give you a tasty bright red sauce which will keep for about two weeks. This sauce may also be made with dark berries and black currant jelly. It can be spiked with raspberry liqueur or kirsch.

Prepare this sauce one day in advance.

MAKES 2 CUPS

1 cup	ripe strawberries
1 cup	ripe raspberries
½ cup	red currants
¼ cup	icing sugar
1 cup	red currant jelly
1	lemon

SERVING SUGGESTION
Serve this with ice cream, tart fruit or bittersweet chocolate desserts. It's also a good base for summer sherbet drinks or margaritas.

1. Clean berries (if possible, do not wash) and remove stems and leaves. Place berries in a ceramic bowl and top with icing sugar and jelly and the juice of one lemon. Cover and chill in refrigerator for 24 hours.

2. In a food processor, blender or food mill process mixture to a fine purée. Strain sauce into a jar or container with a tight seal and refrigerate.

INDEX